Exam overview

Associated certification

Cisco Certified Support Technician (CCST) Networking

The Cisco Certified Support Technician (CCST) Networking certification validates an individual's skills and knowledge of entry-level networking concepts and topics. The certification demonstrates foundational knowledge and skills needed to show how networks operate, including the devices, media, and protocols that enable network communications.

The Cisco Certified Support Technician (CCST) Networking certification is also a first step toward CCNA certification.

Cisco Certified Support Technician (CCST) Networking Exam

Exam Description

To earn your **CCST Networking** certification, you must pass the exam. This 50-minute exam tests your knowledge of:

| Standards and Concepts | Addressing and Subnet Formats | Endpoints and Media Types | Infrastructure | Diagnosing Problems | Security |

1.0 Standards and Concepts ⌄

2.0 Addressing and Subnet Formats ⌄

3.0 Endpoints and Media Types ⌄

4.0 Infrastructure ⌄

5.0 Diagnosing Problems ⌄

6.0 Security ⌄

compare FTP (File Transfer Protocol), TFTP (Trivial File Transfer Protocol), and STP (Spanning Tree Protocol):

FTP (File Transfer Protocol):

Question 1: What is FTP used for, and how does it work? Answer: FTP is used for transferring files between a client and a server over a network. It operates on the client-server model, where the client initiates a connection to the server using control and data channels. The control channel manages commands and responses, while the data channel transfers actual file data.

Question 2: What security mechanisms does FTP offer for data transfer? Answer: Traditional FTP doesn't provide inherent security mechanisms. FTPS (FTP Secure) and SFTP (SSH File Transfer Protocol) are secure variations that use encryption and secure authentication methods to protect data during transfer.

TFTP (Trivial File Transfer Protocol):

Question 1: How does TFTP differ from FTP? Answer: TFTP is a simplified version of FTP, designed for quick and lightweight file transfers. Unlike FTP, TFTP doesn't use a control channel for commands, and it lacks many of the advanced features of FTP. TFTP is commonly used in scenarios where simplicity and low overhead are more important than advanced functionality.

Question 2: What are some common use cases for TFTP? Answer: TFTP is often used for tasks like booting diskless workstations, updating firmware on network devices, and transferring configuration files to network devices during initial setup.

STP (Spanning Tree Protocol):

Question 1: What is the purpose of STP in networking? Answer: STP is used in Ethernet networks to prevent loops in a network topology, which could lead to broadcast storms and network congestion. STP helps ensure a loop-free, redundant topology by designating one switch as the root bridge and blocking redundant links.

Question 2: How does STP determine which links to block in a looped network? Answer: STP uses Bridge Protocol Data Units (BPDU) to exchange information between switches. Each switch assigns a Bridge ID, and the switch with the lowest Bridge ID becomes the root bridge. STP then selects the best path to the root bridge and blocks redundant paths to prevent loops.

Question 3: Are there any limitations or concerns related to STP? Answer: STP convergence time can be slow, leading to network downtime during topology changes. Rapid Spanning Tree Protocol (RSTP) and Multiple Spanning Tree Protocol (MSTP) were introduced to address some of these limitations and improve convergence times.

Please note that these questions and answers provide a high-level comparison of FTP, TFTP, and STP. Further understanding may require more in-depth study of each protocol and its specific features, use cases, and configurations.

NOTE : TFTP doesn't have authentication mechanisme

---

electromagnetic interference (EMI)/radio frequency (RF), fiber optics, copper cables, and coaxial cables:

EMI/RF:

Question 1: What is Electromagnetic Interference (EMI)? Answer: Electromagnetic Interference (EMI) refers to the disturbance caused by electromagnetic radiation from external sources, affecting the performance of electronic devices or systems. EMI can result in signal degradation, data corruption, or even complete device failure.

Question 2: How can you mitigate EMI in electronic systems? Answer: EMI can be mitigated by using shielding materials, proper grounding, ferrite beads, and placing adequate distance between sensitive components. Additionally, adhering to electromagnetic compatibility (EMC) standards helps reduce EMI effects.

Fiber Optics:

Question 1: What are the main advantages of fiber optic cables over traditional copper cables? Answer: Fiber optic cables offer higher bandwidth, longer transmission distances, immunity to EMI/RFI, and greater data security due to their light-based transmission. They are also thinner and lighter than copper cables.

Question 2: How do fiber optic cables transmit data? Answer: Fiber optic cables use light signals for data transmission. They employ total internal reflection to guide light pulses along the core of the cable, which is made of glass or plastic. The light pulses represent the data being transmitted.

Copper Cables:

Question 1: What are some common types of copper cables used in networking? Answer: Common types of copper cables include Unshielded Twisted Pair (UTP) cables, Shielded Twisted Pair (STP) cables, and Coaxial cables. UTP is widely used for Ethernet connections, while STP offers additional shielding against EMI. Coaxial cables are often used for cable television and broadband internet.

Question 2: What is the difference between UTP and STP cables? Answer: UTP cables have twisted pairs of wires but lack additional shielding. STP cables have both twisted pairs and additional shielding, providing better protection against EMI/RFI. This makes STP more suitable for environments with higher levels of interference.

Coaxial Cables:

Question 1: How does a coaxial cable work for signal transmission? Answer: Coaxial cables have a central conductor surrounded by an insulating layer, a metallic shield, and an outer insulating layer. The central conductor carries the signal, while the outer metallic shield acts as a return path and also provides shielding against EMI.

Question 2: Where are coaxial cables commonly used? Answer: Coaxial cables are commonly used for cable television (CATV) distribution, broadband internet connections, and connections between certain types of network equipment. They offer good performance and are more resistant to EMI compared to unshielded cables.

Please remember that these answers provide a basic overview of the concepts related to EMI/RF, fiber optics, copper cables, and coaxial cables. For a deeper understanding, it's recommended to study these topics in more detail using reputable resources and materials.

1

✅ Your answer is correct!   ⟵ Back   Next ⟶

A new network administrator wants to ensure all of the IP addresses assigned to devices on an internal network are private IP addresses. Which of the following IP addresses is a private IP address? (Choose two)

	Yes	No
172.31.31.31	⊘	
192.168.0.1	⊘	
1.1.1.1		⊘
224.1.1.1		⊘

Explanation:

Private IP addresses are in the following ranges:

10.0.0.0 to 10.255.255.255

172.16.0.0 to 172.31.255.255

192.168.0.1 to 192.168.255.255

Thus, 172.31.31.31 is a private IP address and so is 192.168.0.1.

1.1.1.1 is a public IP address.

224.1.1.1 is a multicast IP address.

2

✓ **Your answer is correct!**   ⟵ Back   Next ⟶

A network administrator needs to configure internal networking on a switch to where 10 ports are used to connect devices in the sales department and 10 ports are used to connect devices in the operations department. What should the administrator configure to fulfill these network requirements?

MAC address filtering

Layer 3 switching

MAC address table

◉ VLAN ✓

Explanation:

A virtual local area network (VLAN) allows for multiple networks to be created on the same switch and then ports can be assigned to those VLANs. Thus, to create an environment with two separate networks on the same switch, one should create VLANs.

A MAC address table stores MAC addresses switch ports find as connections are made to a switch.

MAC address filtering controls the MAC addresses allowed on a switch.

Layer 3 switching involves using routing functions on a switch.

3

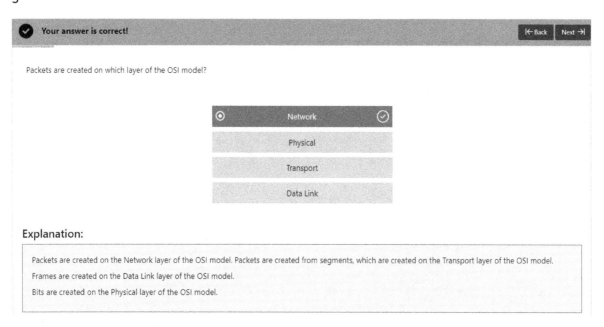

✓ **Your answer is correct!**   ⟵ Back   Next ⟶

Packets are created on which layer of the OSI model?

◉ Network ✓

Physical

Transport

Data Link

Explanation:

Packets are created on the Network layer of the OSI model. Packets are created from segments, which are created on the Transport layer of the OSI model.

Frames are created on the Data Link layer of the OSI model.

Bits are created on the Physical layer of the OSI model.

Refer to the exhibit. A network engineer has configured NATing to allow the PC to communicate with the server.

Which address is the inside global address?

Exhibit   ✕

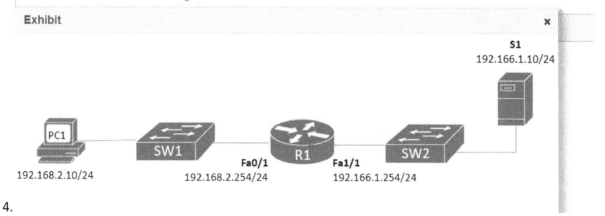

4.

Choose the correct answer

○ 192.166.1.10/24

○ 192.168.2.254/24

○ 192.166.1.254/24

○ 192.168.2.10/24

∧ **Explanation**

The inside global address is 192.166.1.254/24. Network address translation (NAT) lets local nodes with private IP addresses access the internet. In the NAT configuration, the engineer specifies a pool of public IP addresses on the network's edge router. When a local node sends a packet destined for the internet, NATing will map a public IP address from the pool to the packet's source private IP address in a translation table. The packet's source address field is altered to the assigned public IP address and routed normally. The packet's original private source address is called the inside local address. The assigned public IP address is called the inside global address. The engineer can configure NAT overload, which is also called port address

5.

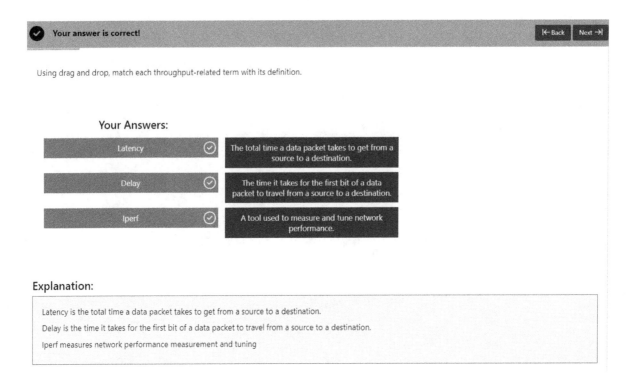

✓ **Your answer is correct!**   ⟵ Back   Next ⟶

Using drag and drop, match each throughput-related term with its definition.

Your Answers:

Latency ✓	The total time a data packet takes to get from a source to a destination.
Delay ✓	The time it takes for the first bit of a data packet to travel from a source to a destination.
Iperf ✓	A tool used to measure and tune network performance.

Explanation:

Latency is the total time a data packet takes to get from a source to a destination.

Delay is the time it takes for the first bit of a data packet to travel from a source to a destination.

Iperf measures network performance measurement and tuning

6

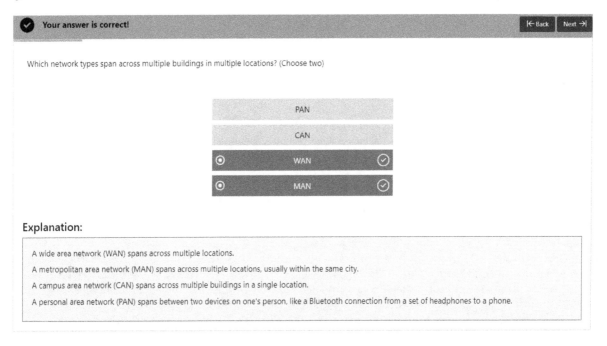

✓ **Your answer is correct!**   ⟵ Back   Next ⟶

Which network types span across multiple buildings in multiple locations? (Choose two)

PAN
CAN
⦿ WAN ✓
⦿ MAN ✓

Explanation:

A wide area network (WAN) spans across multiple locations.

A metropolitan area network (MAN) spans across multiple locations, usually within the same city.

A campus area network (CAN) spans across multiple buildings in a single location.

A personal area network (PAN) spans between two devices on one's person, like a Bluetooth connection from a set of headphones to a phone.

7.

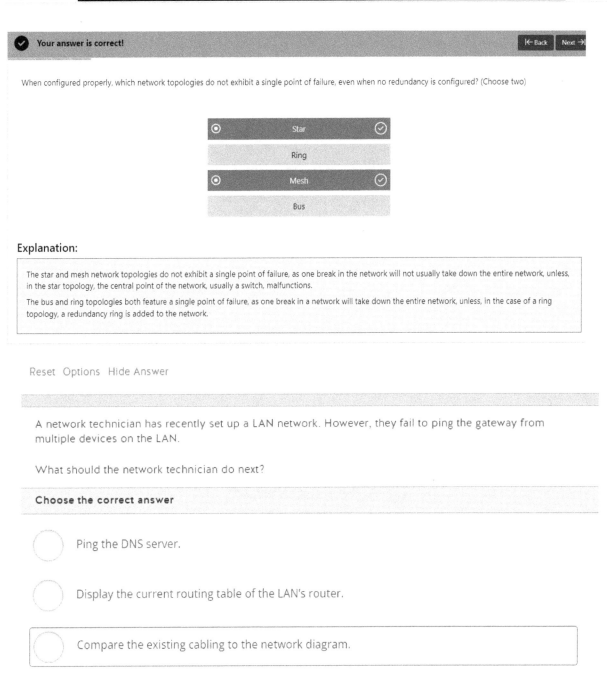

✔ Your answer is correct! |← Back   Next →|

When configured properly, which network topologies do not exhibit a single point of failure, even when no redundancy is configured? (Choose two)

◉ Star ⊘

Ring

◉ Mesh ⊘

Bus

Explanation:

The star and mesh network topologies do not exhibit a single point of failure, as one break in the network will not usually take down the entire network, unless, in the star topology, the central point of the network, usually a switch, malfunctions.

The bus and ring topologies both feature a single point of failure, as one break in a network will take down the entire network, unless, in the case of a ring topology, a redundancy ring is added to the network.

Reset Options Hide Answer

A network technician has recently set up a LAN network. However, they fail to ping the gateway from multiple devices on the LAN.

What should the network technician do next?

Choose the correct answer

○ Ping the DNS server.

○ Display the current routing table of the LAN's router.

○ Compare the existing cabling to the network diagram.

○ Check the ISP's internet connectivity.

8.

∧ **Explanation**

The network technician should compare the existing cabling to the network diagram. Failing pings indicate an issue that resides in the lower three Open Standard Interconnection (OSI) layers, including the physical layer. By comparing the existing cabling to the network diagram, the network technician may discover cables that are misplaced.

The network technician should not ping the Domain Name System (DNS) server. Failed pings indicate issues in the lower three OSI layers. The DNS is a layer seven protocol.

The network technician should not check the Internet Service Provider (ISP)'s internet connectivity. The network technician failed to ping the gateway. The issue resides in the Local Area Network (LAN) that has been recently set up.

The network technician should not display the current routing table of the LAN's router. The gateway is the interface of the router that faces the LAN. No routing is involved in successful pings.

9.

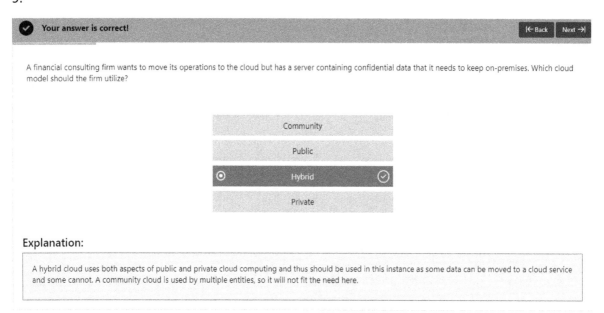

Explanation:

A hybrid cloud uses both aspects of public and private cloud computing and thus should be used in this instance as some data can be moved to a cloud service and some cannot. A community cloud is used by multiple entities, so it will not fit the need here.

10.

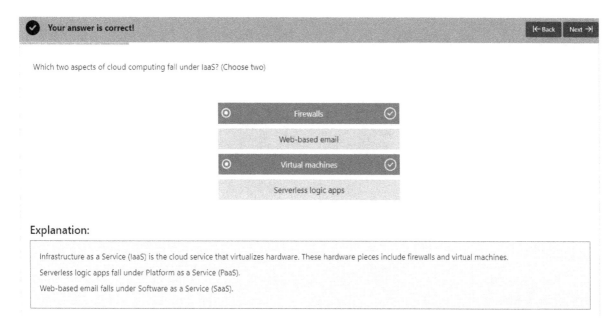

Explanation:

Infrastructure as a Service (IaaS) is the cloud service that virtualizes hardware. These hardware pieces include firewalls and virtual machines.

Serverless logic apps fall under Platform as a Service (PaaS).

Web-based email falls under Software as a Service (SaaS).

11.

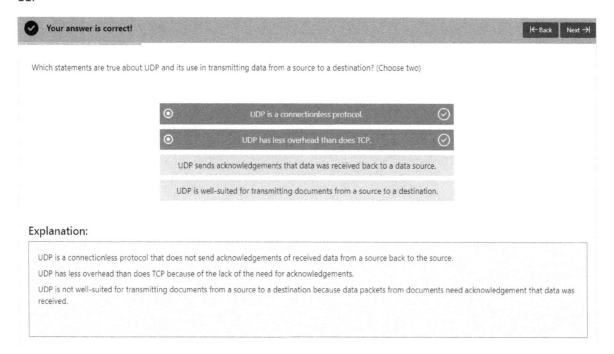

Explanation:

UDP is a connectionless protocol that does not send acknowledgements of received data from a source back to the source.

UDP has less overhead than does TCP because of the lack of the need for acknowledgements.

UDP is not well-suited for transmitting documents from a source to a destination because data packets from documents need acknowledgement that data was received.

12.

|← Back   Next →|

✓ **Your answer is correct!**

A new network administrator is learning about the different ways in which files are transferred from a server to a client machine. Which statements are true regarding FTP? (Choose two)

⦿ Data can be transferred both from a server to a client machine and from a client machine to a server.	✓
⦿ FTP can require authentication.	✓
Data transferred over FTP is secure.	
FTP runs on port 69.	

Explanation:

File Transfer Protocol (FTP) is an unsecure method for transferring files to and from a server. Data transferred via FTP is not encrypted.

Authentication can be required for FTP.

FTP runs on ports 20 and 21. TFTP runs on port 69.

Which two ports on a network device are used to forward user data? (Choose two.)

Choose the correct answers

◯ Fiber ports

◯ Serial ports

◯ AUX ports

◯ Console ports

13.
◯ USB ports

14.

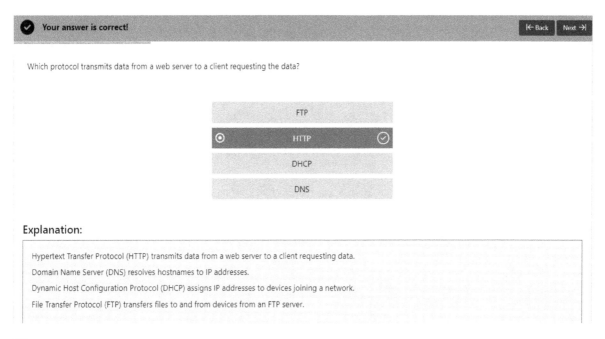

Explanation:

Hypertext Transfer Protocol (HTTP) transmits data from a web server to a client requesting data.

Domain Name Server (DNS) resolves hostnames to IP addresses.

Dynamic Host Configuration Protocol (DHCP) assigns IP addresses to devices joining a network.

File Transfer Protocol (FTP) transfers files to and from devices from an FTP server.

15.

Which network protocol prevents one from having to memorize the IP address of each website they visit?

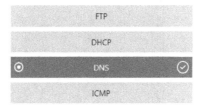

Explanation:

Domain Name Server (DNS) resolves hostnames to IP addresses and IP addresses to hostnames. Thus, DNS prevents one from having to memorize the IP address of each website that a person visits.

Dynamic Host Configuration Protocol (DHCP) assigns IP addresses to hosts.

Internet Control Message Protocol (ICMP) is used to troubleshoot connections to IP addresses and hosts.

File Transfer Protocol (FTP) transfers files between hosts.

16.

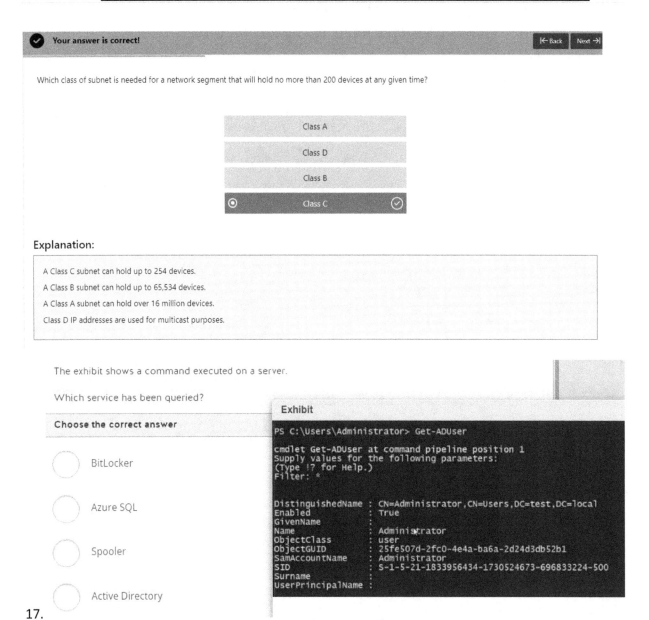

✔ **Your answer is correct!** |← Back   Next →|

Which class of subnet is needed for a network segment that will hold no more than 200 devices at any given time?

| Class A |
| Class D |
| Class B |
| ⊙ Class C   ⊘ |

Explanation:

A Class C subnet can hold up to 254 devices.

A Class B subnet can hold up to 65,534 devices.

A Class A subnet can hold over 16 million devices.

Class D IP addresses are used for multicast purposes.

The exhibit shows a command executed on a server.

Which service has been queried?

Choose the correct answer

○ BitLocker

○ Azure SQL

○ Spooler

○ Active Directory

Exhibit

```
PS C:\Users\Administrator> Get-ADUser

cmdlet Get-ADUser at command pipeline position 1
Supply values for the following parameters:
(Type !? for Help.)
Filter: *


DistinguishedName : CN=Administrator,CN=Users,DC=test,DC=local
Enabled           : True
GivenName         :
Name              : Administrator
ObjectClass       : user
ObjectGUID        : 25fe507d-2fc0-4e4a-ba6a-2d24d3db52b1
SamAccountName    : Administrator
SID               : S-1-5-21-1833956434-1730524673-696833224-500
Surname           :
UserPrincipalName :
```

17.

○ Active Directory

⟍ Explanation

The service that has been queried with the command GET-ADUser is Active Directory. The Get-ADUser command is used in PowerShell to retrieve information about an Active Directory (AD) user and it displays the information in the console output. AD is a Microsoft directory service that manages permissions and controls access to network resources.

Azure Structured Query Language (SQL) has not been queried with the Get-ADUser command as Get-ADUser is a PowerShell cmdlet designed to query Active Directory, not SQL servers. Azure is a cloud computing platform and set of services provided by Microsoft.

Spooler has not been queried with the Get-ADUser command. The Spooler service is related to printing and not AD user management.

BitLocker has not been queried with the Get-ADUser command. BitLocker is a drive encryption feature in Windows and is not related to user management in Active Directory.

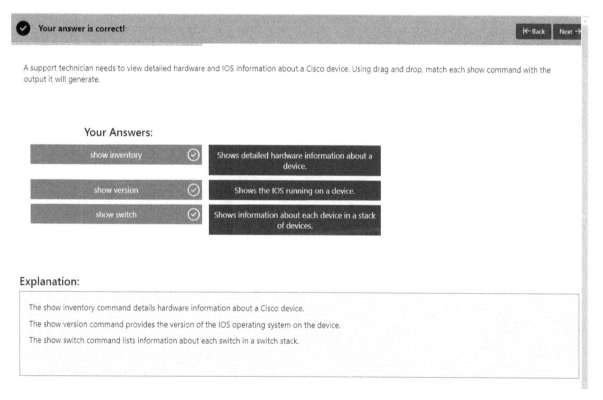

A support technician needs to view detailed hardware and IOS information about a Cisco device. Using drag and drop, match each show command with the output it will generate.

Your Answers:

show inventory ⊘	Shows detailed hardware information about a device.
show version ⊘	Shows the IOS running on a device.
show switch ⊘	Shows information about each device in a stack of devices.

Explanation:

The show inventory command details hardware information about a Cisco device.

The show version command provides the version of the IOS operating system on the device.

The show switch command lists information about each switch in a switch stack.

18.

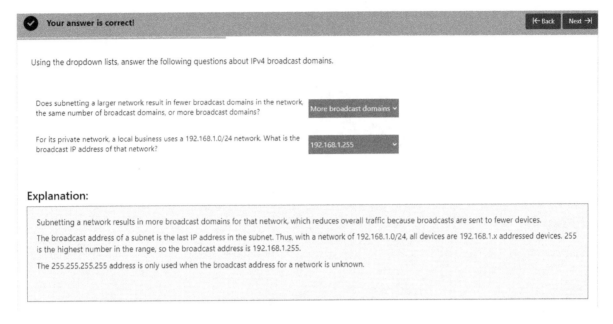

Your answer is correct!
|← Back   Next →|

Using the dropdown lists, answer the following questions about IPv4 broadcast domains.

Does subnetting a larger network result in fewer broadcast domains in the network, the same number of broadcast domains, or more broadcast domains?

More broadcast domains ⌄

For its private network, a local business uses a 192.168.1.0/24 network. What is the broadcast IP address of that network?

192.168.1.255 ⌄

Explanation:

Subnetting a network results in more broadcast domains for that network, which reduces overall traffic because broadcasts are sent to fewer devices.

The broadcast address of a subnet is the last IP address in the subnet. Thus, with a network of 192.168.1.0/24, all devices are 192.168.1.x addressed devices. 255 is the highest number in the range, so the broadcast address is 192.168.1.255.

The 255.255.255.255 address is only used when the broadcast address for a network is unknown.

16

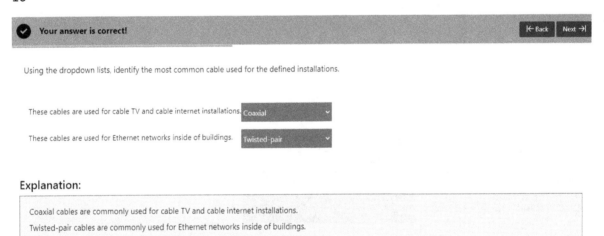

Your answer is correct!
|← Back   Next →|

Using the dropdown lists, identify the most common cable used for the defined installations.

These cables are used for cable TV and cable internet installations. Coaxial ⌄

These cables are used for Ethernet networks inside of buildings. Twisted-pair ⌄

Explanation:

Coaxial cables are commonly used for cable TV and cable internet installations.

Twisted-pair cables are commonly used for Ethernet networks inside of buildings.

Fiber cables are normally used for high-speed, long-distance network connections.

Move the correct VPN type to its corresponding description.

Drag and drop the answers

Remote-access VPN	The secure connection is dynamically created.
Site-to-site VPN	Internal users do not need to install any VPN software.
Site-to-site VPN	VPN gateways are preconfigured to establish a secure tunnel.
Remote-access VPN	It is suitable for connecting work-from-home employees.

19.

20.

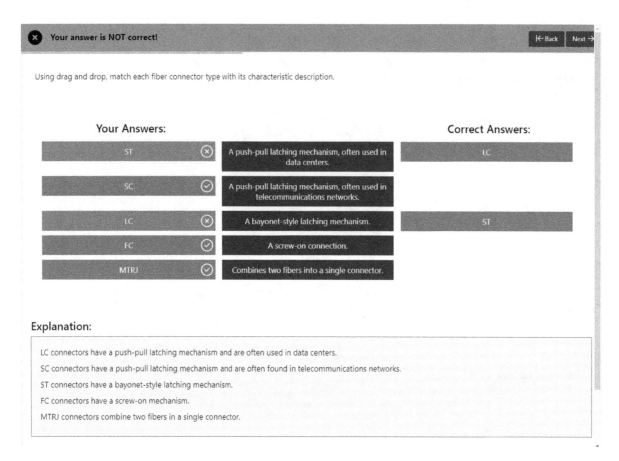

Using drag and drop, match each fiber connector type with its characteristic description.

Explanation:

LC connectors have a push-pull latching mechanism and are often used in data centers.

SC connectors have a push-pull latching mechanism and are often found in telecommunications networks.

ST connectors have a bayonet-style latching mechanism.

FC connectors have a screw-on mechanism.

MTRJ connectors combine two fibers in a single connector.

21.

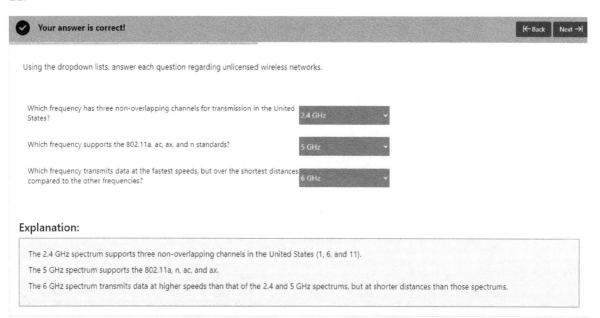

Using the dropdown lists, answer each question regarding unlicensed wireless networks.

Explanation:

The 2.4 GHz spectrum supports three non-overlapping channels in the United States (1, 6, and 11).

The 5 GHz spectrum supports the 802.11a, n, ac, and ax.

The 6 GHz spectrum transmits data at higher speeds than that of the 2.4 and 5 GHz spectrums, but at shorter distances than those spectrums.

Refer to the exhibit. The network technician notices that the given Protocol Data Unit (PDU) never reaches its destination.

What is the reason behind this behavior?

Choose the correct answer

○ The source address belongs to the RFC 1918 IP address ranges.

○ The ICMP code equals zero.

○ The TTL equals one.

○ The differentiated services field equals zero.

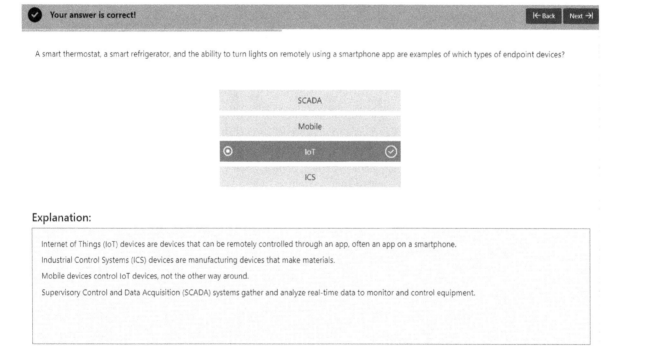

23.

✔ Your answer is correct! |← Back   Next →|

A smart thermostat, a smart refrigerator, and the ability to turn lights on remotely using a smartphone app are examples of which types of endpoint devices?

| SCADA |
| Mobile |
| **IoT** |
| ICS |

Explanation:

Internet of Things (IoT) devices are devices that can be remotely controlled through an app, often an app on a smartphone.

Industrial Control Systems (ICS) devices are manufacturing devices that make materials.

Mobile devices control IoT devices, not the other way around.

Supervisory Control and Data Acquisition (SCADA) systems gather and analyze real-time data to monitor and control equipment.

20

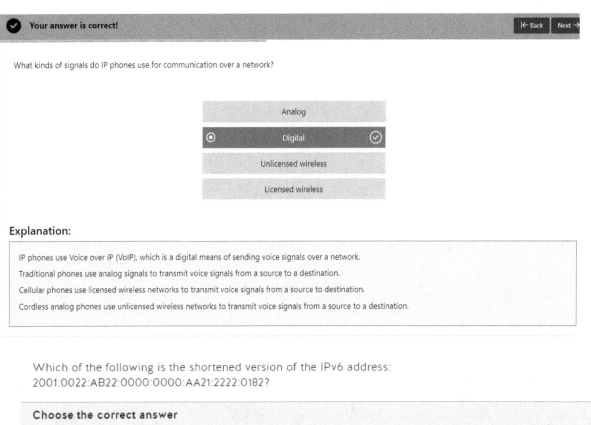

Your answer is correct!

⟵ Back   Next ⟶

What kinds of signals do IP phones use for communication over a network?

- Analog
- ⊙ Digital ✓
- Unlicensed wireless
- Licensed wireless

Explanation:

IP phones use Voice over IP (VoIP), which is a digital means of sending voice signals over a network.

Traditional phones use analog signals to transmit voice signals from a source to a destination.

Cellular phones use licensed wireless networks to transmit voice signals from a source to destination.

Cordless analog phones use unlicensed wireless networks to transmit voice signals from a source to a destination.

Which of the following is the shortened version of the IPv6 address: 2001:0022:AB22:0000:0000:AA21:2222:0182?

Choose the correct answer

◯ 2001:22:AB22:AA21:2222:0182

◯ 2001:22:AB22::AA21:2222::182

◯ 2001:22:AB22::AA21:2222:182

◯ 2001:22:AB22:0000:AA21:2222::

24.

Explanation

The correct shortened version of the 2001:0022:AB22:0000:0000:AA21:2222:0182 IPv6 address is: 2001:22:AB22::AA21:2222:182.

When shortening IPv6 addresses, you can omit leading zeros and any consecutive blocks of zeros. The two consecutive blocks of zeros (0000:0000) can be replaced with a double colon (::). You can only use the double colon once in an IPv6 address. IPv6 addresses are comprised of 128 bits, which are arranged in eight sections.

2001:22:AB22::AA21:2222::182 is incorrect because it contains two sets of double colons and this is not allowed in an IPv6 address.

2001:22:AB22:0000:AA21:2222:: is not correct because it includes double colons at the end, where they are not needed. Only consecutive blocks of zeros can be replaced with a double colon.

2001:22:AB22:AA21:2222:0182 is not a valid IPv6 address. A complete IPv6 address consists of eight sections, and in this example, only six have been provided.

25.

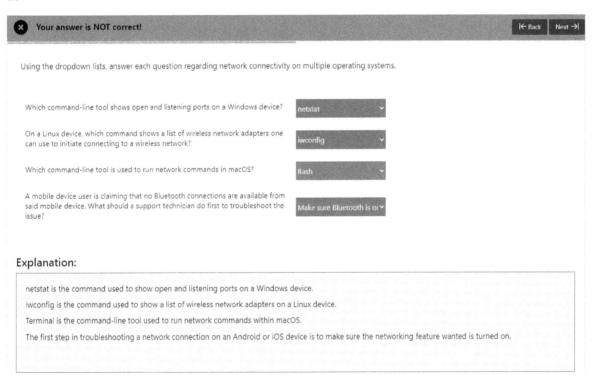

Explanation:

netstat is the command used to show open and listening ports on a Windows device.

iwconfig is the command used to show a list of wireless network adapters on a Linux device.

Terminal is the command-line tool used to run network commands within macOS.

The first step in troubleshooting a network connection on an Android or iOS device is to make sure the networking feature wanted is turned on.

26.

A support technician has been tasked with building a small topology for a company network. What is included in a small topology? (Choose two)

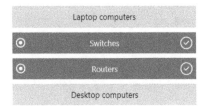

Explanation:

Small topologies should be easy to read. Therefore, only major devices, such as servers, switches, and routers are often included in small topologies.

Desktop and laptop computers are typically not included in small topologies.

A user needs to install hardware for closing roller blinds.

Which of the following devices should the network support technician recommend?

Choose the correct answer

◯ IoT sensor

◯ IoT actuator

◯ IoT DAS

◯ IoT microprocessor

27.

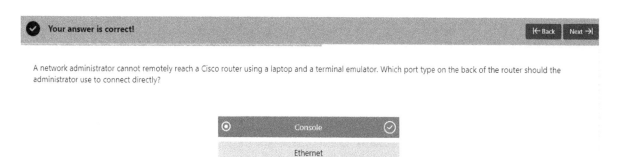

|← Back   Next →|

✔ **Your answer is correct!**

A network administrator cannot remotely reach a Cisco router using a laptop and a terminal emulator. Which port type on the back of the router should the administrator use to connect directly?

⊙	Console	✔
	Ethernet	
	PoE	
	Serial	

Explanation:

A console port allows for a direct connection between a device, such as a laptop or desktop, and a Cisco device, such as a router or switch.

Serial ports allow for one to use serial cables to connect devices such as one router to another.

An Ethernet port does not always allow for one to use a terminal emulator to connect to a device.

Power over Ethernet (PoE) provides power, but not a terminal-based connection to a device.

28.

✔ **Your answer is correct!** |← Back   Next →|

A network administrator is trying to best utilize the Ethernet ports on a switch to provide the highest speeds to devices that need it the most. What is the top speed for a Fast Ethernet port on a Cisco switch?

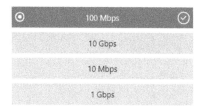

⊙	100 Mbps	✔
	10 Gbps	
	10 Mbps	
	1 Gbps	

Explanation:

A Fast Ethernet port on a Cisco switch has a top speed of 100 Mbps.

Gigabit Ethernet ports have top speeds of 1 Gbps.

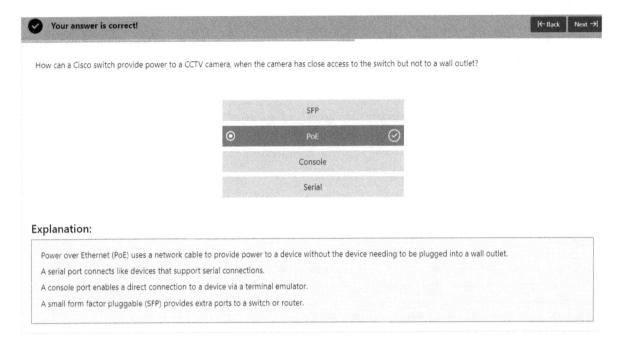

Explanation:

Power over Ethernet (PoE) uses a network cable to provide power to a device without the device needing to be plugged into a wall outlet.

A serial port connects like devices that support serial connections.

A console port enables a direct connection to a device via a terminal emulator.

A small form factor pluggable (SFP) provides extra ports to a switch or router.

26

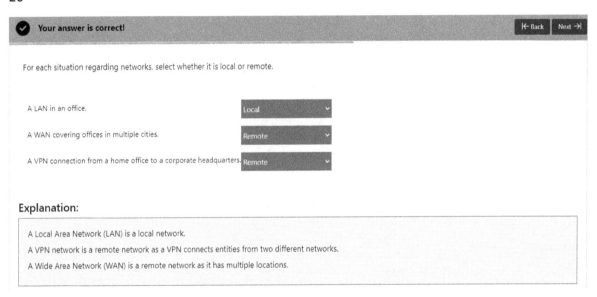

Explanation:

A Local Area Network (LAN) is a local network.

A VPN network is a remote network as a VPN connects entities from two different networks.

A Wide Area Network (WAN) is a remote network as it has multiple locations.

27

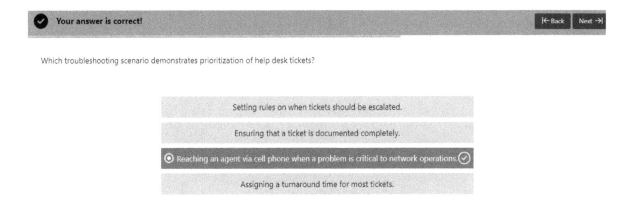

Which troubleshooting scenario demonstrates prioritization of help desk tickets?

Setting rules on when tickets should be escalated.

Ensuring that a ticket is documented completely.

⊙ Reaching an agent via cell phone when a problem is critical to network operations. ✓

Assigning a turnaround time for most tickets.

Explanation:

Prioritization of help desk tickets involves assigning them priorities such as high, normal, or low and then taking action based on priority level.

Prioritization does not involve policy making such as turnaround time for tickets, escalating tickets, or the manner in which a ticket is documented.

28

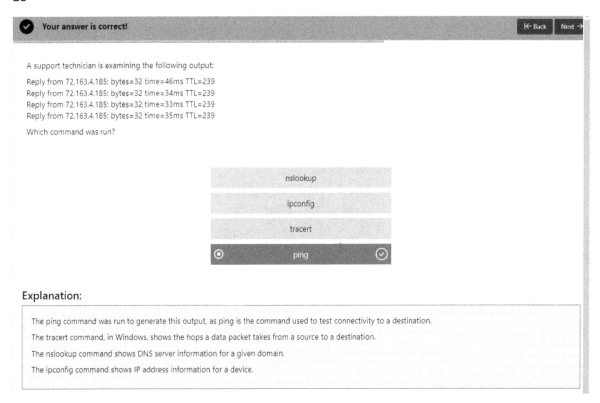

Your answer is correct!

A support technician is examining the following output:

Reply from 72.163.4.185: bytes=32 time=46ms TTL=239
Reply from 72.163.4.185: bytes=32 time=34ms TTL=239
Reply from 72.163.4.185: bytes=32 time=33ms TTL=239
Reply from 72.163.4.185: bytes=32 time=35ms TTL=239

Which command was run?

nslookup

ipconfig

tracert

⊙ ping ✓

Explanation:

The ping command was run to generate this output, as ping is the command used to test connectivity to a destination.

The tracert command, in Windows, shows the hops a data packet takes from a source to a destination.

The nslookup command shows DNS server information for a given domain.

The ipconfig command shows IP address information for a device.

29

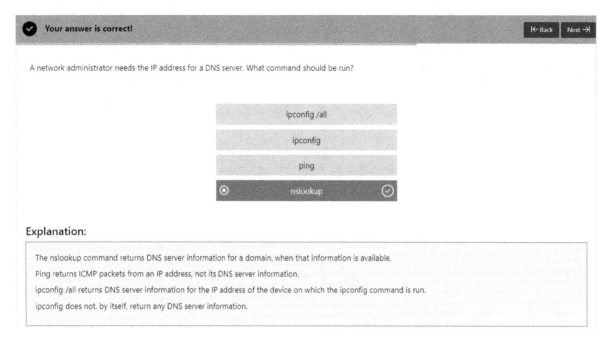

A network administrator needs the IP address for a DNS server. What command should be run?

- ipconfig /all
- ipconfig
- ping
- ● nslookup ✓

Explanation:

The nslookup command returns DNS server information for a domain, when that information is available.

Ping returns ICMP packets from an IP address, not its DNS server information.

ipconfig /all returns DNS server information for the IP address of the device on which the ipconfig command is run.

ipconfig does not, by itself, return any DNS server information.

30

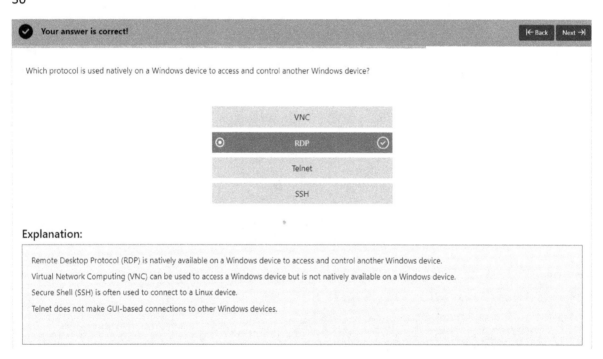

Which protocol is used natively on a Windows device to access and control another Windows device?

- VNC
- ● RDP ✓
- Telnet
- SSH

Explanation:

Remote Desktop Protocol (RDP) is natively available on a Windows device to access and control another Windows device.

Virtual Network Computing (VNC) can be used to access a Windows device but is not natively available on a Windows device.

Secure Shell (SSH) is often used to connect to a Linux device.

Telnet does not make GUI-based connections to other Windows devices.

31

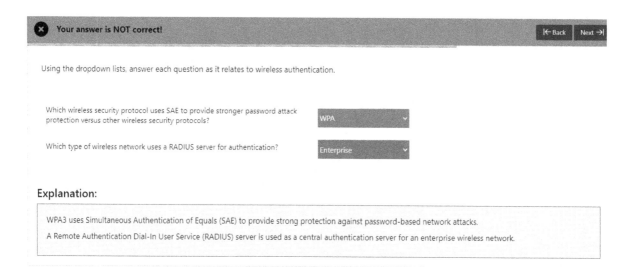

❌ **Your answer is NOT correct!** |← Back   Next →|

Using the dropdown lists, answer each question as it relates to wireless authentication.

Which wireless security protocol uses SAE to provide stronger password attack protection versus other wireless security protocols?   [WPA ▾]

Which type of wireless network uses a RADIUS server for authentication?   [Enterprise ▾]

Explanation:

WPA3 uses Simultaneous Authentication of Equals (SAE) to provide strong protection against password-based network attacks.

A Remote Authentication Dial-In User Service (RADIUS) server is used as a central authentication server for an enterprise wireless network.

32

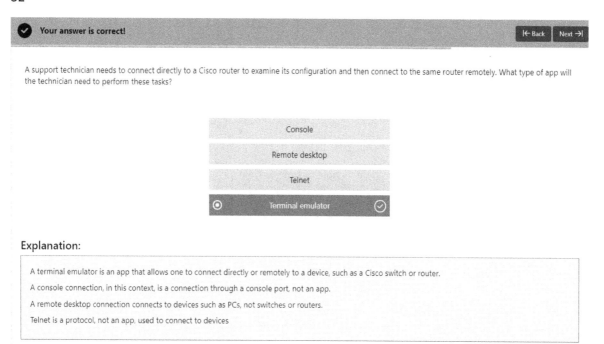

✅ **Your answer is correct!** |← Back   Next →|

A support technician needs to connect directly to a Cisco router to examine its configuration and then connect to the same router remotely. What type of app will the technician need to perform these tasks?

Console

Remote desktop

Telnet

◉ Terminal emulator ✓

Explanation:

A terminal emulator is an app that allows one to connect directly or remotely to a device, such as a Cisco switch or router.

A console connection, in this context, is a connection through a console port, not an app.

A remote desktop connection connects to devices such as PCs, not switches or routers.

Telnet is a protocol, not an app, used to connect to devices

33

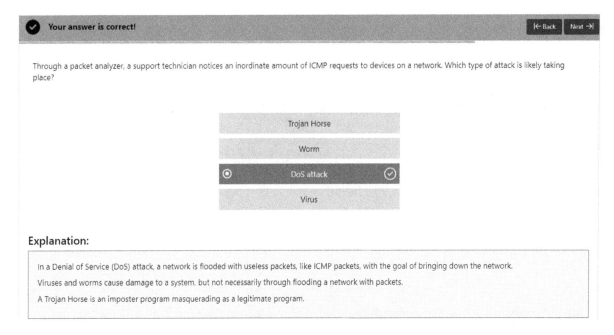

Through a packet analyzer, a support technician notices an inordinate amount of ICMP requests to devices on a network. Which type of attack is likely taking place?

- Trojan Horse
- Worm
- ◉ DoS attack ⊘
- Virus

Explanation:

In a Denial of Service (DoS) attack, a network is flooded with useless packets, like ICMP packets, with the goal of bringing down the network.

Viruses and worms cause damage to a system, but not necessarily through flooding a network with packets.

A Trojan Horse is an imposter program masquerading as a legitimate program.

34

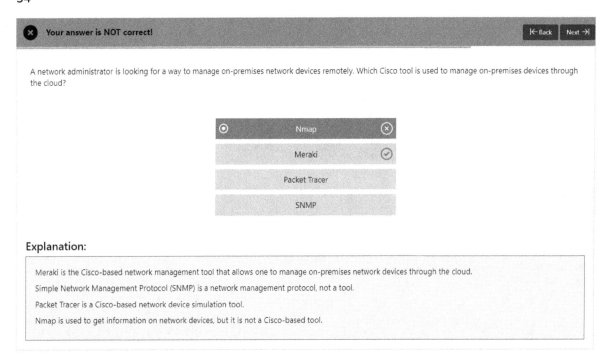

A network administrator is looking for a way to manage on-premises network devices remotely. Which Cisco tool is used to manage on-premises devices through the cloud?

- ◉ Nmap ⊗
- Meraki ⊘
- Packet Tracer
- SNMP

Explanation:

Meraki is the Cisco-based network management tool that allows one to manage on-premises network devices through the cloud.

Simple Network Management Protocol (SNMP) is a network management protocol, not a tool.

Packet Tracer is a Cisco-based network device simulation tool.

Nmap is used to get information on network devices, but it is not a Cisco-based tool.

35

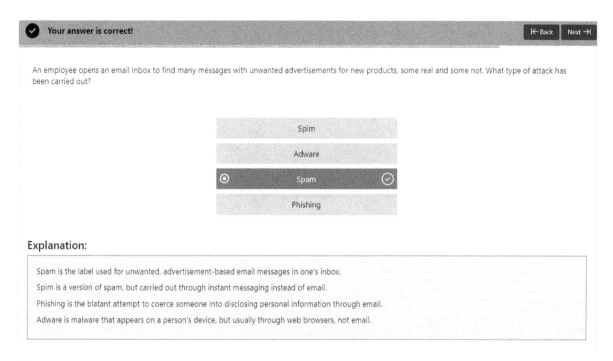

An employee opens an email inbox to find many messages with unwanted advertisements for new products, some real and some not. What type of attack has been carried out?

- Spim
- Adware
- ⦿ Spam ✓
- Phishing

Explanation:

Spam is the label used for unwanted, advertisement-based email messages in one's inbox.

Spim is a version of spam, but carried out through instant messaging instead of email.

Phishing is the blatant attempt to coerce someone into disclosing personal information through email.

Adware is malware that appears on a person's device, but usually through web browsers, not email.

36

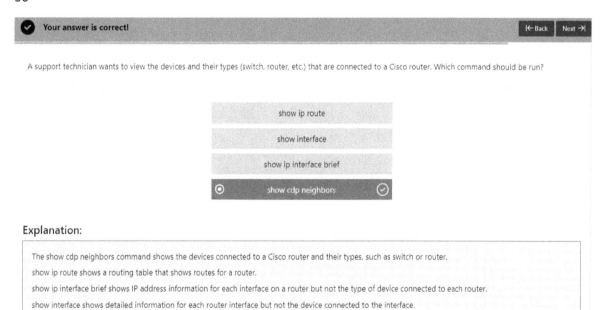

A support technician wants to view the devices and their types (switch, router, etc.) that are connected to a Cisco router. Which command should be run?

- show ip route
- show interface
- show ip interface brief
- ⦿ show cdp neighbors ✓

Explanation:

The show cdp neighbors command shows the devices connected to a Cisco router and their types, such as switch or router.

show ip route shows a routing table that shows routes for a router.

show ip interface brief shows IP address information for each interface on a router but not the type of device connected to each router.

show interface shows detailed information for each router interface but not the device connected to the interface.

37

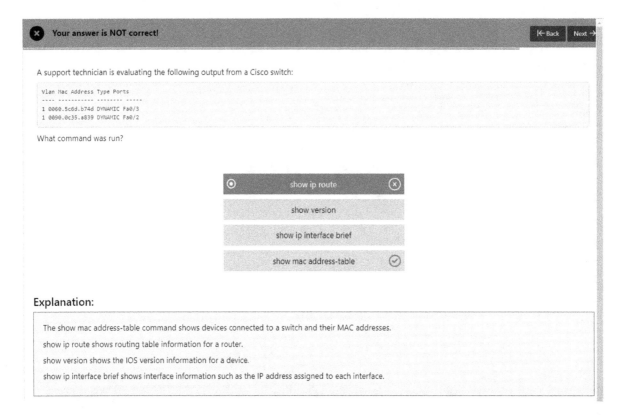

A support technician is evaluating the following output from a Cisco switch:

```
Vlan Mac Address Type Ports
---- ----------- -------- -----
1 0060.5c6d.b74d DYNAMIC Fa0/3
1 0090.0c35.a839 DYNAMIC Fa0/2
```

What command was run?

- ● show ip route ✕
- show version
- show ip interface brief
- show mac address-table ✓

Explanation:

The show mac address-table command shows devices connected to a switch and their MAC addresses.

show ip route shows routing table information for a router.

show version shows the IOS version information for a device.

show ip interface brief shows interface information such as the IP address assigned to each interface.

38

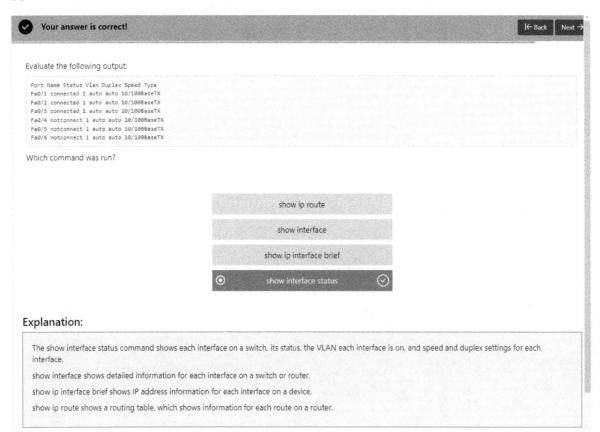

Evaluate the following output:

```
Port Name Status Vlan Duplex Speed Type
Fa0/1 connected 1 auto auto 10/100BaseTX
Fa0/2 connected 1 auto auto 10/100BaseTX
Fa0/3 connected 1 auto auto 10/100BaseTX
Fa0/4 notconnect 1 auto auto 10/100BaseTX
Fa0/5 notconnect 1 auto auto 10/100BaseTX
Fa0/6 notconnect 1 auto auto 10/100BaseTX
```

Which command was run?

- show ip route
- show interface
- show ip interface brief
- ● show interface status ✓

Explanation:

The show interface status command shows each interface on a switch, its status, the VLAN each interface is on, and speed and duplex settings for each interface.

show interface shows detailed information for each interface on a switch or router.

show ip interface brief shows IP address information for each interface on a device.

show ip route shows a routing table, which shows information for each route on a router.

39

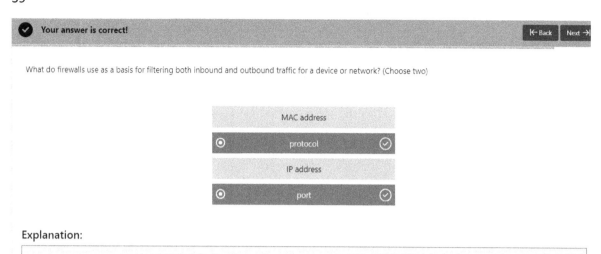

What do firewalls use as a basis for filtering both inbound and outbound traffic for a device or network? (Choose two)

Explanation:

Firewalls use ports and protocols as a basis for filtering both inbound and outbound traffic for a device or network.

Firewalls do not use IP or MAC addresses as a primary means of filtering inbound and outbound traffic for a device or network. Those filters are found primarily on an allow list or block list.

40

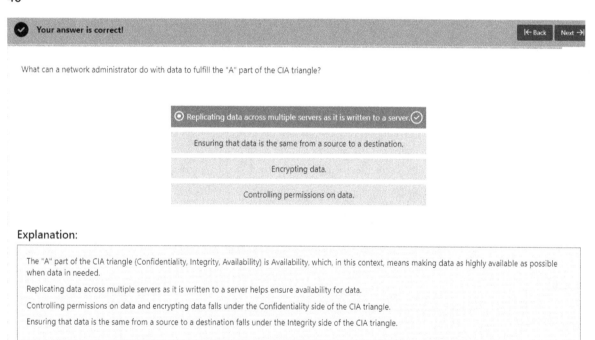

What can a network administrator do with data to fulfill the "A" part of the CIA triangle?

Explanation:

The "A" part of the CIA triangle (Confidentiality, Integrity, Availability) is Availability, which, in this context, means making data as highly available as possible when data in needed.

Replicating data across multiple servers as it is written to a server helps ensure availability for data.

Controlling permissions on data and encrypting data falls under the Confidentiality side of the CIA triangle.

Ensuring that data is the same from a source to a destination falls under the Integrity side of the CIA triangle.

41

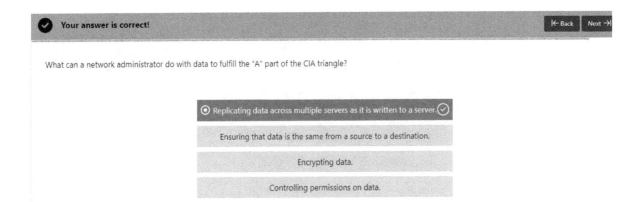

✓ **Your answer is correct!** |← Back   Next →|

What can a network administrator do with data to fulfill the "A" part of the CIA triangle?

⦿ Replicating data across multiple servers as it is written to a server. ✓

Ensuring that data is the same from a source to a destination.

Encrypting data.

Controlling permissions on data.

Explanation:

The "A" part of the CIA triangle (Confidentiality, Integrity, Availability) is Availability, which, in this context, means making data as highly available as possible when data in needed.

Replicating data across multiple servers as it is written to a server helps ensure availability for data.

Controlling permissions on data and encrypting data falls under the Confidentiality side of the CIA triangle.

Ensuring that data is the same from a source to a destination falls under the Integrity side of the CIA triangle.

42

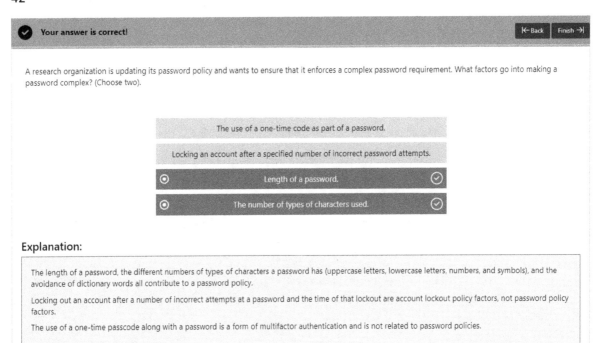

✓ **Your answer is correct!** |← Back   Finish →|

A research organization is updating its password policy and wants to ensure that it enforces a complex password requirement. What factors go into making a password complex? (Choose two).

The use of a one-time code as part of a password.

Locking an account after a specified number of incorrect password attempts.

⦿ Length of a password. ✓

⦿ The number of types of characters used. ✓

Explanation:

The length of a password, the different numbers of types of characters a password has (uppercase letters, lowercase letters, numbers, and symbols), and the avoidance of dictionary words all contribute to a password policy.

Locking out an account after a number of incorrect attempts at a password and the time of that lockout are account lockout policy factors, not password policy factors.

The use of a one-time passcode along with a password is a form of multifactor authentication and is not related to password policies.

questions and answers related to Telnet, RDP (Remote Desktop Protocol), and SSH (Secure Shell):

Telnet:

Question 1: What is Telnet and what is its primary purpose? Answer: Telnet is a network protocol used for remote terminal connections to devices, typically routers, switches, and servers. Its primary purpose is to establish a virtual terminal session on a remote host to manage and configure it.

Question 2: What are some security concerns associated with Telnet? Answer: Telnet sends data, including login credentials, in clear text, making it vulnerable to eavesdropping and unauthorized access. Because of this lack of encryption, Telnet is considered insecure and is often replaced by more secure protocols like SSH.

RDP (Remote Desktop Protocol):

Question 1: What is RDP and how is it used? Answer: RDP (Remote Desktop Protocol) is a proprietary protocol developed by Microsoft for remote access to Windows-based systems. It allows users to remotely control a computer's graphical desktop interface and access applications as if they were physically present at the system.

Question 2: What security measures should be taken when using RDP? Answer: To enhance security when using RDP, it's important to use strong passwords, enable Network Level Authentication (NLA) for enhanced authentication, and consider using a Virtual Private Network (VPN) to encrypt the RDP traffic over the internet.

SSH (Secure Shell):

Question 1: What is SSH and why is it considered more secure than Telnet? Answer: SSH (Secure Shell) is a cryptographic network protocol used for secure remote access and data transfer. Unlike Telnet, SSH encrypts the data exchanged between the client and the server, making it highly secure against eavesdropping and unauthorized access.

Question 2: What are the main components of SSH? Answer: SSH consists of three main components: the client, the server, and the protocol. The client initiates a connection to the server and uses the SSH protocol to establish a secure session for data exchange and remote management.

Question 3: How does public key authentication work in SSH? Answer: Public key authentication in SSH involves generating a key pair: a public key and a private key. The public key is stored on the server, and the corresponding private key is kept securely by the client. During authentication, the client proves its identity by using the private key to sign a challenge from the server. If the server can verify the signature using the stored public key, the client is granted access.

Telnet Scenario: Configuring Network Devices

Scenario: A network administrator needs to remotely configure a router located at a remote office.

Question: Why might Telnet be used for this scenario, and what security concerns should the administrator be aware of? **Answer:** Telnet might be used because it allows remote access to the router's command-line interface for configuration. However, the security concern is that Telnet sends data in clear text, which means that sensitive information, including login credentials, can be intercepted by malicious actors on the network.

SSH Scenario: Remote Server Administration

Scenario: An IT administrator needs to manage a Linux server located in a data center remotely.

Question: How does SSH benefit the IT administrator in this scenario, and what security features does SSH provide? **Answer:** SSH is beneficial because it provides secure remote access to the server's command-line interface. It encrypts data, including login credentials, preventing eavesdropping. SSH also supports key-based authentication, which enhances security by eliminating the need to send passwords over the network.

RDP Scenario: Remote Desktop Support

Scenario: An IT support technician needs to troubleshoot an issue on an employee's computer located in a different office.

Question: How does RDP facilitate remote troubleshooting, and what security measures should the technician take to ensure data security during the session? **Answer:** RDP allows the technician to connect to the employee's desktop remotely, enabling them to diagnose and resolve the issue as if they were sitting at the computer. To ensure data security, the technician should use strong authentication methods, such as requiring complex passwords or enabling Network Level Authentication (NLA). If the connection is over the internet, using a VPN can further encrypt the RDP traffic.

NOTE !

1.For accessing remotely a PC or a Server : RDP

1.For accessing remotely a Switch or a Router for configuration or management : telnet and Ssh

But for a secured or encrypted access use **ssh**

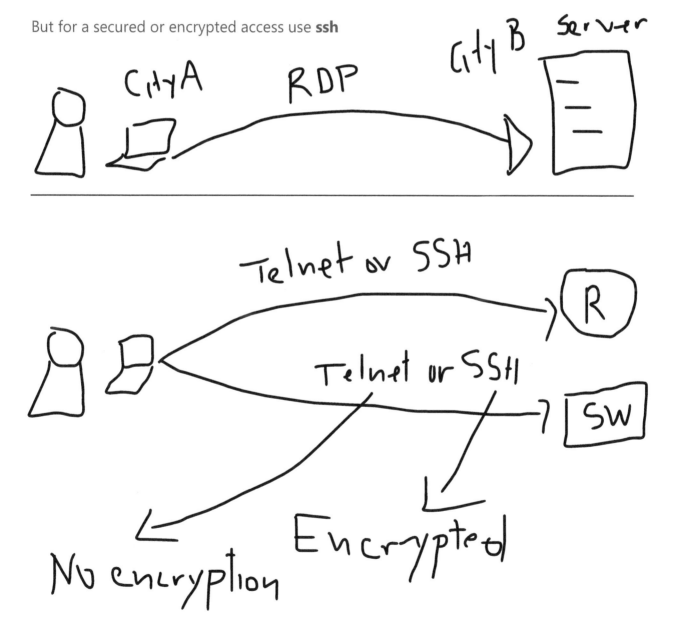

concepts of SaaS (Software as a Service), PaaS (Platform as a Service), and IaaS (Infrastructure as a Service):

SaaS (Software as a Service):

Question 1: What is SaaS? Answer: SaaS stands for Software as a Service. It's a cloud computing model where software applications are delivered over the internet on a subscription basis. Users can access the software through a web browser without needing to install or maintain it locally.

Question 2: What are the benefits of using SaaS? Answer: SaaS offers benefits such as easy accessibility, automatic updates, scalability, and reduced upfront costs. Users don't need to worry about software maintenance, as the service provider handles updates and maintenance.

PaaS (Platform as a Service):

Question 1: What is PaaS? Answer: PaaS stands for Platform as a Service. It provides a platform and environment for developers to build, deploy, and manage applications without managing the underlying infrastructure. PaaS includes tools, libraries, and services to facilitate application development.

Question 2: How does PaaS benefit developers? Answer: PaaS simplifies the development process by offering a pre-configured environment, which reduces the time and effort required to set up infrastructure. Developers can focus more on coding and application logic rather than managing hardware and software components.

IaaS (Infrastructure as a Service):

Question 1: What is IaaS? Answer: IaaS stands for Infrastructure as a Service. It provides virtualized computing resources over the internet, such as virtual machines, storage, and networking. Users can rent these resources on-demand and pay for what they use.

Question 2: What are the advantages of using IaaS? Answer: IaaS offers flexibility, scalability, and cost savings. Users can quickly scale up or down based on their needs without investing in physical hardware. It's suitable for scenarios where custom configurations are required.

Scenario-based Questions:

Scenario: You are a small business owner looking to manage your customer relationships. Which cloud model would be most suitable for you? Answer: SaaS would be most suitable. You can subscribe to a CRM (Customer Relationship Management) SaaS solution, giving you access to the software without the need to manage servers or software updates.

Scenario: You are a developer creating a web application and want to focus on coding rather than managing the underlying infrastructure. Which cloud model should you consider? Answer: PaaS would be ideal. It provides you with the platform and tools necessary for application development, allowing you to concentrate on coding, deployment, and scaling.

Scenario: Your company needs to set up a new development and testing environment quickly for a short-term project. Which cloud model would provide the necessary resources? Answer: IaaS would be suitable. You can provision virtual machines and storage resources as needed for the development and testing period, and then decommission them after the project is complete.

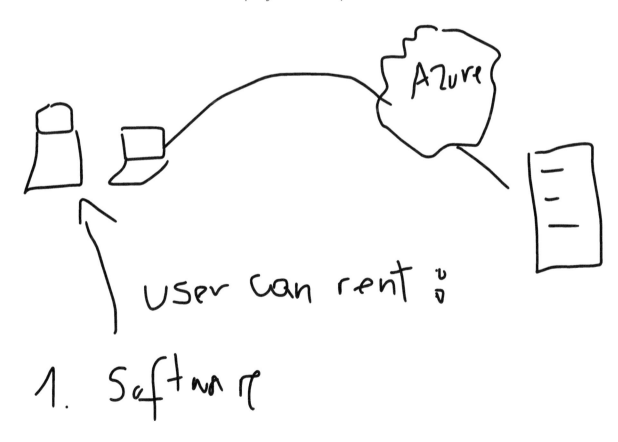

2. Virtual devices (VM, VSw,...)

3. Environment to develop apps

Latency:

Question 1: What is latency in networking? Answer: Latency refers to the time delay between sending a data packet from its source to its destination and receiving a response back. It is often measured in milliseconds (ms) and is influenced by factors like the distance between endpoints, network congestion, and processing times.

Question 2: How does latency impact network performance? Answer: High latency can lead to delays in data transmission and response times, which can affect real-time applications like online gaming, VoIP, and video conferencing. Low-latency networks are crucial for smooth user experiences in such applications.

Question 3: What are some factors that contribute to latency? Answer: Latency can be affected by factors such as physical distance, network congestion, router processing times, and the quality of network infrastructure. Light travels faster through fiber-optic cables compared to copper cables, which can reduce latency.

Bandwidth:

Question 1: What is bandwidth in networking? Answer: Bandwidth refers to the maximum data transfer rate of a network connection. It is usually measured in bits per second (bps) and indicates how much data can be transmitted within a given time frame.

Question 2: How does bandwidth affect data transfer? Answer: Higher bandwidth allows for faster data transfer rates, enabling more data to be transmitted in a shorter period. Applications like streaming, file downloads, and cloud services benefit from higher bandwidth connections.

Question 3: Can high bandwidth guarantee low latency? Answer: No, high bandwidth does not necessarily guarantee low latency. While higher bandwidth can accommodate more data, latency depends on factors like network congestion, routing, and the physical distance between endpoints.

Latency vs. Bandwidth:

Question 1: How are latency and bandwidth related? Answer: Latency and bandwidth are related but distinct concepts. While bandwidth represents the capacity for data transmission, latency focuses on the time it takes for data to travel from source to destination. A high-bandwidth connection can carry more data, but if latency is high, it might still experience delays.

Question 2: In which scenarios is latency more critical than bandwidth? Answer: Latency is more critical in scenarios that require real-time interactions, such as online gaming, video conferencing, and remote control applications. In these cases, even a high-bandwidth connection with significant latency can result in a poor user experience.

Question 3: In which scenarios is bandwidth more critical than latency? Answer: Bandwidth is more critical in scenarios involving large data transfers, such as streaming high-definition videos, downloading large files, and backups. A high-bandwidth connection ensures efficient transfer of large volumes of data.

$$\text{Latency} = \text{Total time}$$

S → msg → DEST

Tt = 5 Sec

Total time for the msg to go from Source to destination

When latency increases, it does not directly affect the bandwidth itself. Latency and bandwidth are related but distinct concepts in networking.

- **Latency:** As mentioned earlier, latency refers to the time delay between sending a data packet from its source to its destination and receiving a response back. It is often measured in milliseconds (ms). Latency is influenced by factors such as distance, network congestion, processing times, and the quality of the network infrastructure.
- **Bandwidth:** Bandwidth, on the other hand, refers to the maximum data transfer rate of a network connection. It indicates how much data can be transmitted within a given time frame, usually measured in bits per second (bps).

Increasing latency does not directly affect the bandwidth capacity itself. However, high latency can lead to delays in data transmission and response times. Applications that require real-time interactions, such as online gaming or video conferencing, can be affected negatively by high latency because the delay between sending a command or message and receiving a response becomes noticeable and can hinder smooth interactions.

While latency and bandwidth are separate concepts, they can collectively impact the performance of network applications. A high-bandwidth connection might be able to transmit a large amount of data, but if latency is high, there may still be noticeable delays in transmitting and receiving that data. It's essential to consider both latency and bandwidth when assessing network performance for different types of applications.

questions and answers related to SNMP (Simple Network Management Protocol):

Question 1: What is SNMP? Answer: SNMP stands for Simple Network Management Protocol. It is a widely used protocol for managing and monitoring network devices, such as routers, switches, servers, and printers. SNMP allows network administrators to collect information about the health, performance, and status of devices in a network.

Question 2: What are the main components of SNMP? Answer: SNMP involves three main components:

1. **Managed Devices:** These are the network devices being monitored and managed. They contain SNMP agents, which collect and store information about the device.

2. **SNMP Agents:** Agents are software modules residing on managed devices. They collect data and respond to SNMP queries from a central management station.
3. **Management Stations:** These are systems used by network administrators to monitor and manage devices. Management stations send SNMP queries to agents to gather information.

Question 3: What is an SNMP Community String? Answer: An SNMP community string is like a password that acts as a shared secret between an SNMP manager and an SNMP agent. It is included in SNMP messages to authenticate and authorize requests from the manager. There are two types of community strings: read-only (RO) for querying information and read-write (RW) for modifying configurations.

Question 4: What are SNMP MIBs? Answer: MIB stands for Management Information Base. It is a database that contains a hierarchical collection of managed object definitions. MIBs define the structure of the data that can be accessed through SNMP. MIBs provide a standardized way to represent and manage network device information.

Question 5: What are the SNMP versions, and how do they differ? Answer: SNMP has several versions, including SNMPv1, SNMPv2c, and SNMPv3:

- SNMPv1: The original version with basic functionality but limited security features.
- SNMPv2c: An improved version with enhancements but still lacks robust security.
- SNMPv3: The most secure version, introducing features like authentication, encryption, and user-based access control.

Question 6: What are SNMP traps? Answer: SNMP traps are unsolicited messages sent from an SNMP agent to a management station to notify about specific events, such as device failures or critical conditions. Traps provide real-time alerts to network administrators.

Question 7: How is SNMP used for network management? Answer: SNMP is used for various network management tasks, including monitoring device health, collecting performance statistics, configuring device parameters, and receiving real-time notifications about network events.

Question 8: What is the default SNMP port? Answer: The default SNMP port is 161 for receiving SNMP queries (GET requests) and 162 for receiving SNMP traps (unsolicited messages).

Question 9: How can SNMP security be enhanced in SNMPv3? Answer: SNMPv3 introduced security features like authentication and encryption. Administrators can set up usernames, passwords, and encryption keys to secure SNMP communication between management stations and agents.

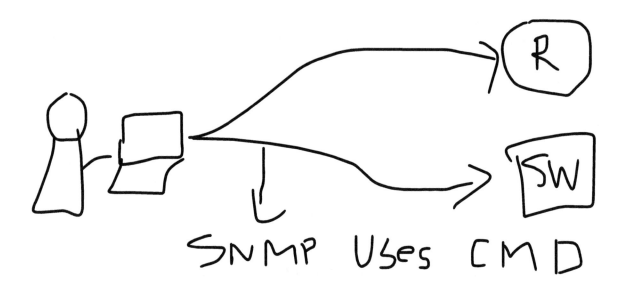

SNMP USes CMD

OSI model

Layer	Name	Example protocols
7	Application Layer	HTTP, FTP, DNS, SNMP, Telnet
6	Presentation Layer	SSL, TLS
5	Session Layer	NetBIOS, PPTP
4	Transport Layer	TCP, UDP
3	Network Layer	IP, ARP, ICMP, IPSec
2	Data Link Layer	PPP, ATM, Ethernet
1	Physical Layer	Ethernet, USB, Bluetooth, IEEE802.11

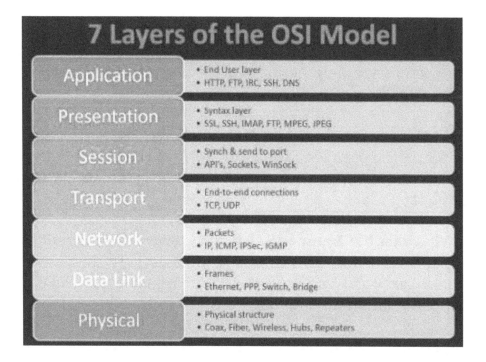

Question 1: What is the OSI model? Answer: The OSI model is a conceptual framework that standardizes the functions of a telecommunication or computing system into seven distinct layers. It was developed by the International Organization for Standardization (ISO) to facilitate communication between different systems and vendors.

Question 2: What are the seven layers of the OSI model, from bottom to top? Answer: The seven layers of the OSI model are:

1. Physical Layer
2. Data Link Layer
3. Network Layer
4. Transport Layer
5. Session Layer
6. Presentation Layer
7. Application Layer

Question 3: What is the purpose of the Physical Layer? Answer: The Physical Layer is responsible for transmitting raw binary data over the physical medium, such as electrical signals over cables or light pulses over fiber optics. It deals with the physical characteristics of the transmission medium and connectors.

Question 4: What does the Data Link Layer do? Answer: The Data Link Layer provides error detection, frame synchronization, and flow control for reliable data transmission between directly connected nodes. It's responsible for creating frames from the raw data provided by the Physical Layer.

Question 5: What is the function of the Network Layer? Answer: The Network Layer is responsible for routing packets of data across different networks. It determines the best path for data to travel from source to destination while considering factors like network topology and addressing.

Question 6: What does the Transport Layer do? Answer: The Transport Layer ensures end-to-end communication and data delivery between devices. It provides error detection, segmentation, and reassembly of data into manageable chunks, as well as flow control and sequencing.

Question 7: What is the purpose of the Session Layer? Answer: The Session Layer establishes, maintains, and terminates communication sessions between two devices. It manages dialog control, allowing for full-duplex or half-duplex communication.

Question 8: What does the Presentation Layer handle? Answer: The Presentation Layer is responsible for data translation, encryption, compression, and formatting. It ensures that data from the Application Layer is presented in a format understandable by the receiving application.

Question 9: What is the role of the Application Layer? Answer: The Application Layer provides a direct interface for end-users and application programs. It includes various application services like email, file transfer, remote access, and web browsing.

Question 10: How does the OSI model aid in networking and communication? Answer: The OSI model provides a common framework for understanding and discussing networking concepts. It helps network engineers and developers design, troubleshoot, and implement network protocols and services across different systems and vendors.

2

✓ **Your answer is correct!** |← Back   Next →|

For each statement on wireless frequencies, indicate Yes if the statement is true and No if the statement is false.

	Yes	No
The 6 GHz frequency has the widest frequency range of the three bands used for WiFi networks.	⊘	
The 2.4 GHz frequency carries a signal the furthest among the three bands used for WiFi networks.	⊘	
The 5 GHz frequency has three non-overlapping channels.		⊘

Explanation:

True statements:

The 6 GHz frequency has the widest frequency range of the three bands used for WiFi networks.

The 2.4 GHz frequency carries a signal the furthest among the three bands used for WiFi networks.

False statements:

The 5 GHz frequency has three non-overlapping channels.

Explanation

The 5 GHz frequency has 24 non-overlapping channels. The 2.4 GHz frequency has three non-overlapping channels.

3

A command output produces the following result:

```
Codes: L - local, C - connected, S - static, R - RIP, M - mobile, B - BGP
D - EIGRP, EX - EIGRP external, O - OSPF, IA - OSPF inter area
N1 - OSPF NSSA external type 1, N2 - OSPF NSSA external type 2
E1 - OSPF external type 1, E2 - OSPF external type 2, E - EGP
i - IS-IS, L1 - IS-IS level-1, L2 - IS-IS level-2, ia - IS-IS inter area
* - candidate default, U - per-user static route, o - ODR
P - periodic downloaded static route

Gateway of last resort is not set

1.0.0.0/32 is subnetted, 1 subnets
C 1.1.1.1 is directly connected, Loopback0
```

Which command was run?

- ◉ show ip route ✓
- show cdp neighbors
- show inventory
- show mac-address-table

Explanation:

The output is a routing table, meaning the show ip route command was run.

show mac-address-table shows MAC addresses that switch ports have learned.

show cdp neighbors shows neighboring devices using the Cisco Discovery Protocol (CDP)

show inventory shows products installed on a device.

Subnet Mask

10.0.0.0/8 ——> 255.0.0.0

192.168.0.2/16 —> 255.255.0.0

192.168.2.4/24 —> 255.255.255.0

⚠️ Master this slash notation

$Ex_2:$ New Subnet.

$192.168.0.0/26$

$26 = 24 + 2$

$255.255.255.\ 1\ 1\ 0\ 0\ 0\ 0\ 0\ 0$

6 Zeros

$128 + 64 = 192$

New Subnet = 255.255.255.192

⚠ Number of host usable

$2^{6 \ Zeros} - 2 = 64 - 2 = 60$

Ex_2 : 192.168.0.3/27

27 = 24 + 3

255.255.255. 1 1 1 0 0 0 0 0

$2^5 - 2 = 30$ → usable host

128 + 64 + 32

255.255.255.224

← New Sub

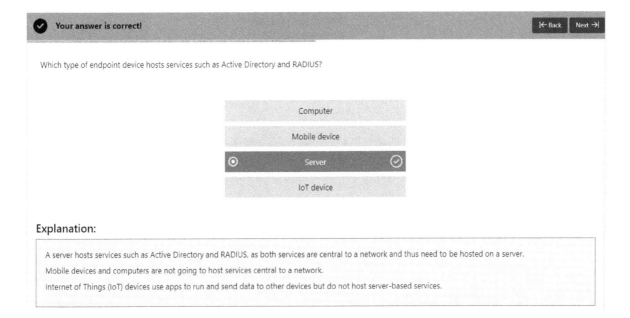

Your answer is correct! |← Back | Next →|

Which type of endpoint device hosts services such as Active Directory and RADIUS?

- Computer
- Mobile device
- ● Server ✓
- IoT device

Explanation:

A server hosts services such as Active Directory and RADIUS, as both services are central to a network and thus need to be hosted on a server.

Mobile devices and computers are not going to host services central to a network.

Internet of Things (IoT) devices use apps to run and send data to other devices but do not host server-based services.

23

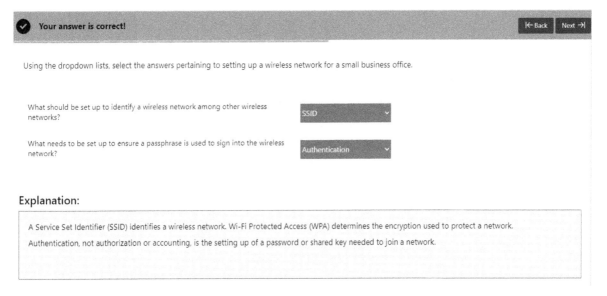

Your answer is correct! |← Back | Next →|

Using the dropdown lists, select the answers pertaining to setting up a wireless network for a small business office.

What should be set up to identify a wireless network among other wireless networks? | SSID ⌄ |

What needs to be set up to ensure a passphrase is used to sign into the wireless network? | Authentication ⌄ |

Explanation:

A Service Set Identifier (SSID) identifies a wireless network. Wi-Fi Protected Access (WPA) determines the encryption used to protect a network.

Authentication, not authorization or accounting, is the setting up of a password or shared key needed to join a network.

24

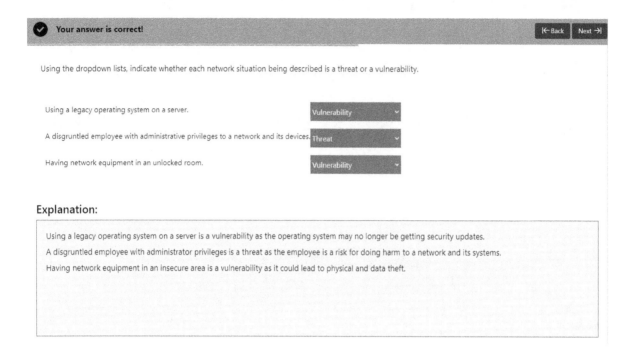

✓ Your answer is correct! |← Back   Next →|

Using the dropdown lists, indicate whether each network situation being described is a threat or a vulnerability.

Using a legacy operating system on a server.   Vulnerability ▼

A disgruntled employee with administrative privileges to a network and its devices. Threat ▼

Having network equipment in an unlocked room.   Vulnerability ▼

Explanation:

Using a legacy operating system on a server is a vulnerability as the operating system may no longer be getting security updates.

A disgruntled employee with administrator privileges is a threat as the employee is a risk for doing harm to a network and its systems.

Having network equipment in an insecure area is a vulnerability as it could lead to physical and data theft.

25

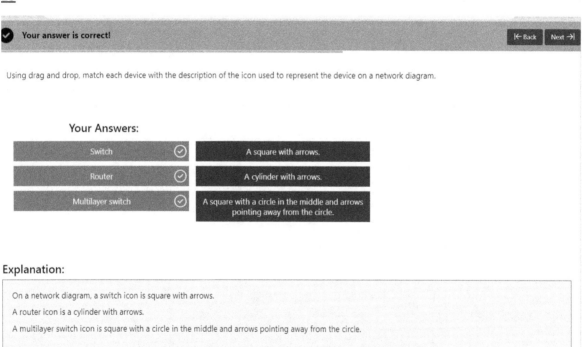

✓ Your answer is correct! |← Back   Next →|

Using drag and drop, match each device with the description of the icon used to represent the device on a network diagram.

Your Answers:

Switch	✓	A square with arrows.
Router	✓	A cylinder with arrows.
Multilayer switch	✓	A square with a circle in the middle and arrows pointing away from the circle.

Explanation:

On a network diagram, a switch icon is square with arrows.

A router icon is a cylinder with arrows.

A multilayer switch icon is square with a circle in the middle and arrows pointing away from the circle.

26

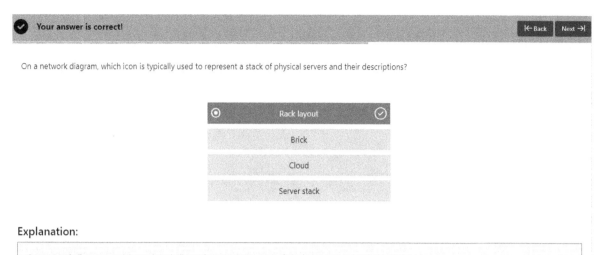

On a network diagram, which icon is typically used to represent a stack of physical servers and their descriptions?

- ⦿ Rack layout ✓
- Brick
- Cloud
- Server stack

Explanation:

On a network diagram, a rack layout is typically used to represent a stack of physical servers and their descriptions.

A cloud is typically used to represent one or more servers in the cloud.

A brick is typically used to represent a firewall.

A stack of servers with no rack usually represents a server pool.

27

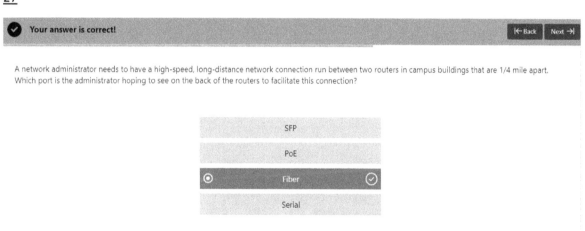

A network administrator needs to have a high-speed, long-distance network connection run between two routers in campus buildings that are 1/4 mile apart. Which port is the administrator hoping to see on the back of the routers to facilitate this connection?

- SFP
- PoE
- ⦿ Fiber ✓
- Serial

Explanation:

For high-speed, long-distance connections, a fiber port is needed on the back of each router.

A small-form factor pluggable (SFP) might contain a fiber port, but an SFP in of itself is not a port.

Power over Ethernet (PoE) provides power but not high-speed connectivity.

Serial ports can initiate longer-distance connections but not at as high of speed as are fiber connections.

28

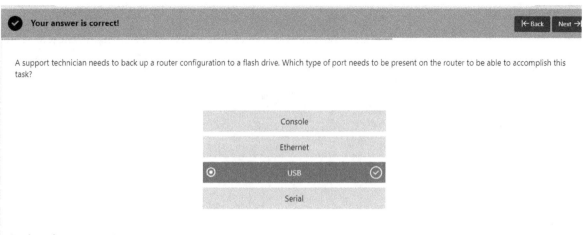

✓ **Your answer is correct!** |← Back   Next →|

A support technician needs to back up a router configuration to a flash drive. Which type of port needs to be present on the router to be able to accomplish this task?

- Console
- Ethernet
- ⦿ USB ✓
- Serial

Explanation:

A Universal Serial Bus (USB) port is the most common port used for flash drives and thus needs to be present on a device to provide a port a flash drive can access.

Serial ports are normally used to connect routers to other routers.

Console ports are used for devices to have direct connections to and configure switches and routers.

An Ethernet port is used to transmit data but flash drives typically do not have an Ethernet port.

29

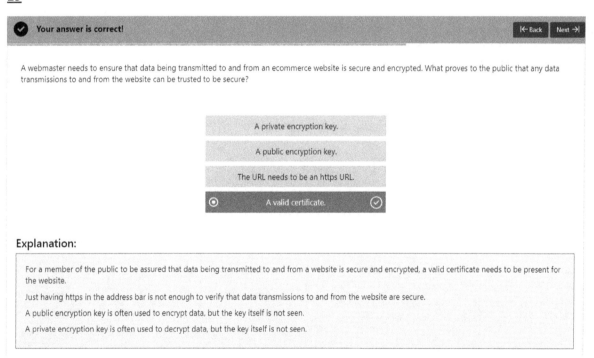

✓ **Your answer is correct!** |← Back   Next →|

A webmaster needs to ensure that data being transmitted to and from an ecommerce website is secure and encrypted. What proves to the public that any data transmissions to and from the website can be trusted to be secure?

- A private encryption key.
- A public encryption key.
- The URL needs to be an https URL.
- ⦿ A valid certificate. ✓

Explanation:

For a member of the public to be assured that data being transmitted to and from a website is secure and encrypted, a valid certificate needs to be present for the website.

Just having https in the address bar is not enough to verify that data transmissions to and from the website are secure.

A public encryption key is often used to encrypt data, but the key itself is not seen.

A private encryption key is often used to decrypt data, but the key itself is not seen.

30

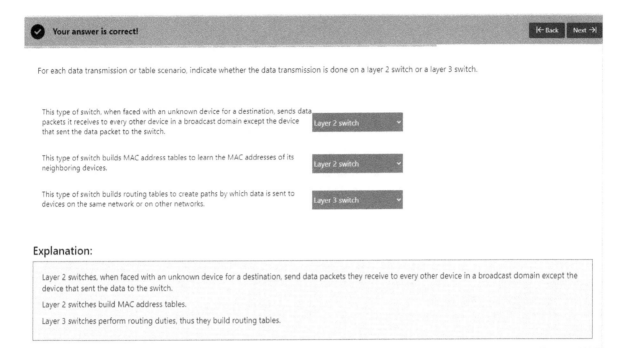

For each data transmission or table scenario, indicate whether the data transmission is done on a layer 2 switch or a layer 3 switch.

This type of switch, when faced with an unknown device for a destination, sends data packets it receives to every other device in a broadcast domain except the device that sent the data packet to the switch. [Layer 2 switch ▾]

This type of switch builds MAC address tables to learn the MAC addresses of its neighboring devices. [Layer 2 switch ▾]

This type of switch builds routing tables to create paths by which data is sent to devices on the same network or on other networks. [Layer 3 switch ▾]

Explanation:

Layer 2 switches, when faced with an unknown device for a destination, send data packets they receive to every other device in a broadcast domain except the device that sent the data to the switch.

Layer 2 switches build MAC address tables.

Layer 3 switches perform routing duties, thus they build routing tables.

<u>31</u>

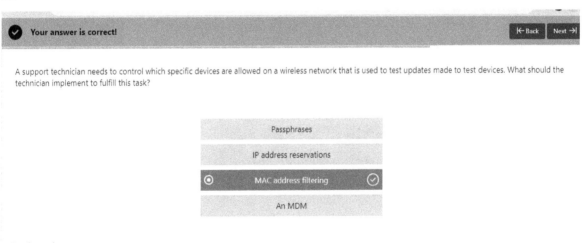

A support technician needs to control which specific devices are allowed on a wireless network that is used to test updates made to test devices. What should the technician implement to fulfill this task?

Passphrases

IP address reservations

◉ MAC address filtering ✓

An MDM

Explanation:

To control which specific devices are allowed on a wireless network, MAC address filtering should be implemented.

Using IP address reservations does not, in itself, limit a device from attempting to get on a network.

Implementing a passphrase does not control which specific devices are allowed on a network as any user with the passphrase can get a device onto the network.

A Mobile Device Management (MDM) tool can control devices by policy but not specify specific allowed devices on a network.

<u>32</u>

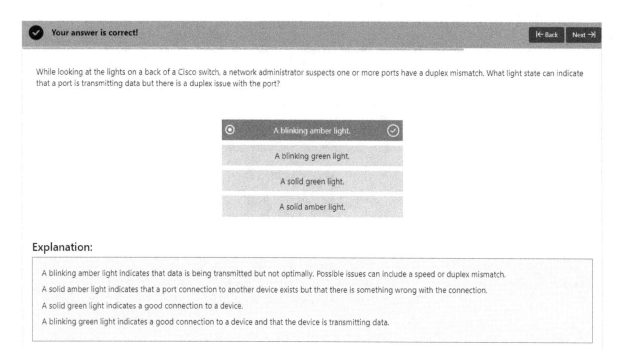

Explanation:

A blinking amber light indicates that data is being transmitted but not optimally. Possible issues can include a speed or duplex mismatch.

A solid amber light indicates that a port connection to another device exists but that there is something wrong with the connection.

A solid green light indicates a good connection to a device.

A blinking green light indicates a good connection to a device and that the device is transmitting data.

33

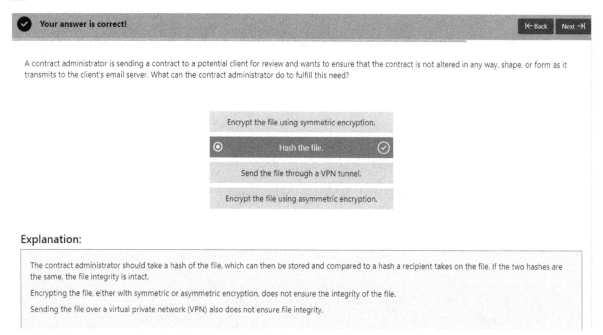

Explanation:

The contract administrator should take a hash of the file, which can then be stored and compared to a hash a recipient takes on the file. If the two hashes are the same, the file integrity is intact.

Encrypting the file, either with symmetric or asymmetric encryption, does not ensure the integrity of the file.

Sending the file over a virtual private network (VPN) also does not ensure file integrity.

34

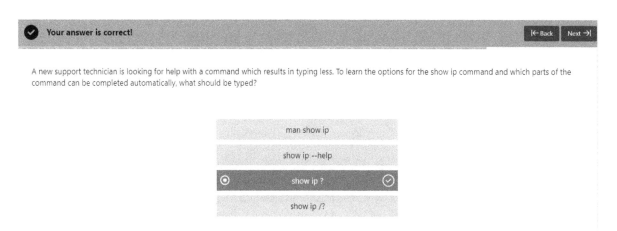

Your answer is correct!

| ← Back | Next → |

A new support technician is looking for help with a command which results in typing less. To learn the options for the show ip command and which parts of the command can be completed automatically, what should be typed?

man show ip

show ip --help

● show ip ?   ⊘

show ip /?

Explanation:

A command and a question mark will show the options one can use with the command. Thus, typing show ip ? shows all the options for the show ip command.

/? gets help for a Windows command.

The man command is used for Linux commands.

--help is also used in Linux commands.

35

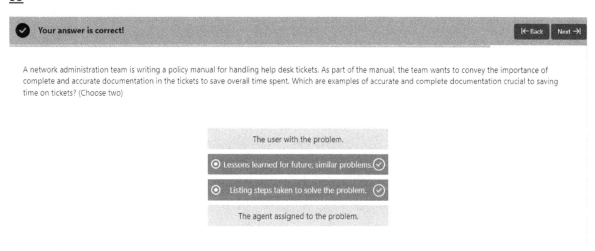

Your answer is correct!

| ← Back | Next → |

A network administration team is writing a policy manual for handling help desk tickets. As part of the manual, the team wants to convey the importance of complete and accurate documentation in the tickets to save overall time spent. Which are examples of accurate and complete documentation crucial to saving time on tickets? (Choose two)

The user with the problem.

⊙ Lessons learned for future, similar problems. ⊘

⊙ Listing steps taken to solve the problem. ⊘

The agent assigned to the problem.

Explanation:

Lessons learned for future, similar problems, and a list of steps taken to solve the problem are crucial documentation pieces for help desk tickets as it relates to saving time spent overall on help desk tickets.

Ensuring the person with the problem and the agent assigned to the ticket are on the ticket are not as critical for saving overall time spent on help desk tickets.

36

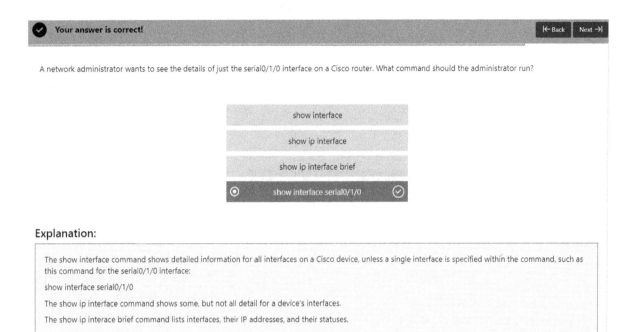

A network administrator wants to see the details of just the serial0/1/0 interface on a Cisco router. What command should the administrator run?

- show interface
- show ip interface
- show ip interface brief
- ⦿ show interface serial0/1/0 ✓

Explanation:

The show interface command shows detailed information for all interfaces on a Cisco device, unless a single interface is specified within the command, such as this command for the serial0/1/0 interface:

show interface serial0/1/0

The show ip interface command shows some, but not all detail for a device's interfaces.

The show ip interace brief command lists interfaces, their IP addresses, and their statuses.

37

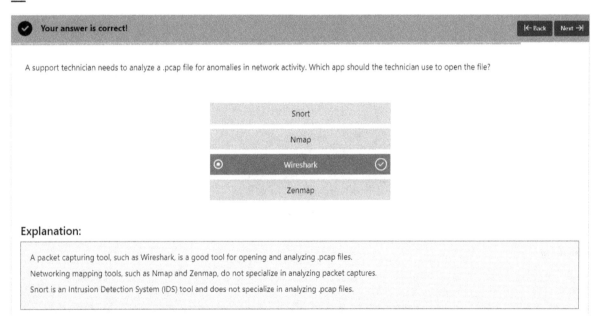

A support technician needs to analyze a .pcap file for anomalies in network activity. Which app should the technician use to open the file?

- Snort
- Nmap
- ⦿ Wireshark ✓
- Zenmap

Explanation:

A packet capturing tool, such as Wireshark, is a good tool for opening and analyzing .pcap files.

Networking mapping tools, such as Nmap and Zenmap, do not specialize in analyzing packet captures.

Snort is an Intrusion Detection System (IDS) tool and does not specialize in analyzing .pcap files.

38

Which command was run?

show start

show license

show run ⊙ ✓

show version

Explanation:

The show run command shows a running configuration on a Cisco device.

The show start command shows a starting configuration on a Cisco device.

The show version command shows the IOS version running a Cisco device.

The show license command shows the licensed products and services on a Cisco device.

39

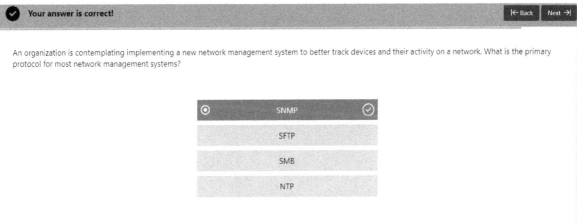

✓ **Your answer is correct!** |← Back   Next →|

An organization is contemplating implementing a new network management system to better track devices and their activity on a network. What is the primary protocol for most network management systems?

SNMP ⊙ ✓

SFTP

SMB

NTP

Explanation:

Network management systems use the Simple Network Management Protocol (SNMP) to communicate with the devices on the network.

Network Time Protocol (NTP) is used to synchronize time across devices on a network.

Server Message Block (SMB) is used to share files from servers to client devices.

Secure File Transfer Protocol (SFTP) is used to transfer files securely between an FTP server and a device.

40

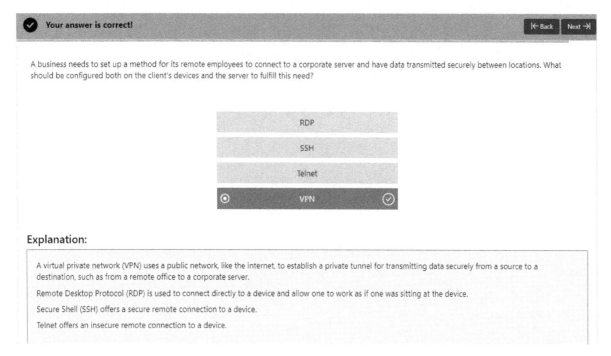

Explanation:

A virtual private network (VPN) uses a public network, like the internet, to establish a private tunnel for transmitting data securely from a source to a destination, such as from a remote office to a corporate server.

Remote Desktop Protocol (RDP) is used to connect directly to a device and allow one to work as if one was sitting at the device.

Secure Shell (SSH) offers a secure remote connection to a device.

Telnet offers an insecure remote connection to a device.

41

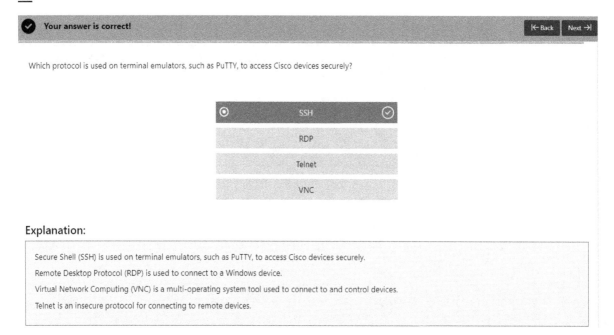

Explanation:

Secure Shell (SSH) is used on terminal emulators, such as PuTTY, to access Cisco devices securely.

Remote Desktop Protocol (RDP) is used to connect to a Windows device.

Virtual Network Computing (VNC) is a multi-operating system tool used to connect to and control devices.

Telnet is an insecure protocol for connecting to remote devices.

42

compare TCP (Transmission Control Protocol) and UDP (User Datagram Protocol):

Question 1: What are TCP and UDP, and how do they differ in terms of connection-oriented vs. connectionless communication?

Answer: TCP and UDP are transport layer protocols used in computer networks to facilitate communication between devices. TCP is a connection-oriented protocol, which means it establishes a reliable, ordered, and error-checked connection before data transmission. UDP, on the other hand, is a connectionless protocol that does not establish a formal connection before sending data. It provides a faster and simpler way to transmit data but does not guarantee reliability or order.

Question 2: How do TCP and UDP handle error checking and retransmission of lost data?

Answer: TCP provides extensive error checking and correction mechanisms. It uses acknowledgments and sequence numbers to ensure that data is delivered reliably and in the correct order. If data is lost or corrupted, TCP will request retransmission from the sender. UDP, however, does not have built-in error checking or retransmission mechanisms. It sends data without guarantees, and any error checking or recovery must be implemented at the application layer.

Question 3: Which protocol is more suitable for applications where real-time data delivery is crucial, such as VoIP and online gaming?

Answer: UDP is more suitable for real-time applications because it offers lower latency and overhead. VoIP (Voice over Internet Protocol) and online gaming prioritize speed over guaranteed delivery, and a small delay in data transmission is often preferred over potential latency introduced by TCP's error recovery mechanisms.

Question 4: In terms of data delivery order, how do TCP and UDP behave?

Answer: TCP guarantees in-order delivery of data packets. It reorders packets at the receiver's end if they arrive out of order. UDP does not guarantee order; packets may arrive out of sequence, and it's the responsibility of the application layer to reorder them if necessary.

Question 5: Which protocol is commonly used for file transfers, such as downloading files from a server?

Answer: TCP is commonly used for file transfers, especially when data integrity and reliability are important. TCP's error recovery and acknowledgment mechanisms ensure that all parts of the file are successfully transferred.

Question 6: How do TCP and UDP handle congestion control?

Answer: TCP has sophisticated congestion control mechanisms to manage network congestion and prevent network congestion collapse. It dynamically adjusts its transmission rate based on network conditions. UDP, however, does not include congestion control. If the network becomes congested, UDP packets may be dropped without any explicit mechanism to slow down the sender.

Question 7: Which protocol is more suitable for applications that require minimal data overhead and acknowledgment delays, such as DNS queries?

Answer: UDP is more suitable for applications that require minimal data overhead and low acknowledgment delays. DNS (Domain Name System) queries, for instance, often use UDP due to its lower latency and simpler packet structure.

some examples that illustrate when TCP (Transmission Control Protocol) or UDP (User Datagram Protocol) would be more appropriate based on different types of applications and their requirements:

Example 1: Web Browsing (HTTP)

TCP is more suitable for web browsing (HTTP) because it requires reliable and ordered data delivery. When you request a webpage, the server sends the content using TCP to ensure that all the elements of the webpage, such as images and text, arrive in the correct order and without errors. This is important to provide a consistent browsing experience.

Example 2: Video Streaming

UDP is commonly used for video streaming. Video streaming applications, like YouTube and Netflix, use UDP because real-time delivery is prioritized over reliability. A small amount of packet loss or out-of-order packets may not significantly affect the viewing experience, and the lower latency provided by UDP is crucial for seamless video playback.

Example 3: Online Gaming

UDP is preferred for online gaming due to its low latency and minimal overhead. Online games require real-time interaction, and delays caused by TCP's acknowledgment and retransmission mechanisms would negatively impact gameplay. UDP allows the game data to arrive quickly, even if some packets are lost.

Example 4: File Transfer (FTP)

TCP is well-suited for file transfers using protocols like FTP (File Transfer Protocol). When downloading large files, data integrity and accuracy are crucial. TCP's error checking, acknowledgment, and retransmission mechanisms ensure that all parts of the file are received correctly.

Example 5: Voice over IP (VoIP)

UDP is commonly used for VoIP applications like Skype and Zoom. Real-time voice communication requires low latency to maintain a natural conversation flow. While some packets may be lost or arrive out of order, the emphasis is on minimizing delays and providing real-time conversation.

Example 6: DNS Queries

UDP is often used for DNS queries. DNS lookups involve sending a query to a DNS server to resolve domain names to IP addresses. These queries are short and require low latency, making UDP an appropriate choice. If a response is lost, the application can quickly resend the query.

1

In a corporate environment, which two devices are most likely to receive a dynamic IP address from a DHCP server? (Choose two.)

Choose the correct answers

( ) Printer

( ) Mobile phone

( ) Laptop

( ) Switch

( ) Server

Devices such as laptops and mobile phones in a corporate environment are typically assigned dynamic IP addresses through Dynamic Host Configuration Protocol (DHCP). DHCP ensures that standard parameters, such as IP addresses, are sent by the server to each device automatically. DHCP is easy to implement and minimizes configuration errors.

Achieving a similar result to assigning a static IP address can be accomplished through DHCP reservations. DHCP reservations associate a device's MAC address with a specific IP address.

Servers are critical components and require static IP addresses to maintain constant accessibility and reachability.

Printers are assigned static IP addresses to ensure consistent connectivity across the entire network.

Switches and other network devices require a static IP address because they serve as fixed points in the network. End users rely on network devices to communicate and exchange data. Unlike devices such as laptops or mobile phones that may frequently connect and disconnect from the network, switches and other network devices are always on and connected.

References

DHCP vs. Static IP in a Digital World: When To Use Each

Static vs. dynamic IP addresses

2

( ) Ctrl-B

( ) Tab

( ) Ctrl-F

( ) Ctrl-E

Explanation

You should press the Tab key to autocomplete a command on a Cisco device. The Cisco command-line interface provides this useful feature, helping to speed up configuration tasks and reduce typing errors.

You should not press Ctrl-E, Ctrl-B, or Ctrl-F to autocomplete a command on a Cisco device. The correct key to press is the Tab key.

Here are some popular shortcuts you can use:

- Ctrl-E - Cursor moves to the end of the line
- Ctrl-B - Cursor moves back one character
- Ctrl-Z - Exit the current mode
- Ctrl-F - Cursor moves forward one character

References

Using the Command-Line Interface

3

Which of the following may interfere with a Wi-Fi signal?

Choose the correct answer

○   STP cables

○   External power lines

○   Coaxial cables

○   Optical fiber cables

Explanation

External power lines create an electromagnetic field that may interfere with Wi-Fi. The interference takes the form of reduced throughput or reduced signal strength.

Shielded Twisted Pair (STP) cables do not cause any significant interference. The electric signal carried in their copper strands creates an electromagnetic field. However, the twisting and shielding prevent the field from being omitted and interfering with Wi-Fi.

Optical fiber cables do not interfere with a Wi-Fi signal. Optical fiber does not create an electromagnetic field, as it relies on sending light pulses on a thin strand of glass.

4

○ Protocol

○ ToS

○ TTL

○ IHL

∧ Explanation

The Type of Service (ToS) is the packet field responsible for Quality of Service (QoS) marking. ToS is one byte long. Its value informs downstream routers how to treat the packet and prioritize its forwarding.

The Internet Header Length (IHL) field is not used for QoS marking. Instead, it represents the number of 32-bit words in the packet's header.

The Time To Live (TTL) field is not used for QoS marking. Instead, it is for mitigating routing loops.

The protocol field is not used for QoS marking. Instead, it is to inform the upper layer the protocol of the packet's payload. Its value can indicate that the payload includes a Transport Control Protocol (TCP), User Datagram Protocol (UDP), or Internet Control Messaging Protocol (ICMP) segment.

References

Anatomy of an IPv4 Packet

5

○ fdff:105a:22cc:3:6350:45ff:fe7b:580c

○ ff0c:106f:22dc::73c1:22ff:fe7c:6e3e

○ fe80:0db8:85b3::8a2e:0380:d334

○ fc00:106b:22dc:48he:6351:434f:ff7b:683b

∧ **Explanation**

fdff:105a:22cc:3:6350:45ff:fe7b:580c can be obtained via the Extended Unique Identifier (EUI) method to be unique within a company. The IPv6 address is 128 bits. The leftmost 64 bits are the network bits configured on the local router interface. The remaining 64 bits are called the interface ID. The EUI method uses the Media Access Control (MAC) address of the device interface to generate the interface ID. The MAC address is 48 bits long. To extend it to 64 bits, 16 bits are inserted in the middle of the MAC value. These 16 bits in hexadecimal are ff:fe. fdff:105a:22cc:3:6350:45ff:fe7b:580c is a unique local address at the company network level because it starts with fdff. The start can be from fc00::/7 to fdff::/7. fdff:105a:22cc:3:6350:45ff:fe7b:580c has the ff:fe bits inserted correctly in the interface ID part.

fe80:0db8:85b3::8a2e:0380:d334 cannot be obtained via the EUI method to be unique within a company. First, this address is a link local address because it starts with fe80::/10. It is unique on the level of the link only. Besides, it cannot be obtained via EUI because it has no ff:fe inserted in the interface ID part.

ff0c:106f:22dc::73c1:22ff:fe7c:6e3e cannot be obtained via the EUI method to be unique within a company. This IPv6 address is a multicast address because it starts with ff::/8 and it is not assignable to an interface.

fc00:106b:22dc:48ba:6351:434f:ff7b:683b cannot be obtained via the EUI method or be unique within a

6. ARP is used for IPV4 and ICMPV6 FOR IPV6

Example 7: IoT Device Communication

UDP can be used for communication with IoT (Internet of Things) devices. Many IoT devices require rapid communication of small amounts of data, and reliability might be less critical than speed. UDP's lower overhead and lower latency are beneficial in this scenario.

In summary, the choice between TCP and UDP depends on the specific needs of the application. TCP provides reliability, ordered data delivery, and error correction, making it suitable for applications where data integrity is essential. UDP prioritizes low latency and speed, making it a good choice for real-time applications where occasional packet loss or out-of-order delivery can be tolerated.

a list of examples of IoT devices, keep in mind that the specific devices available on the market can change over time due to technological advancements and trends. Here's a diverse list of 20 IoT devices that were common as of my last update in September 2021:

1. **Smart Thermostat:** Devices that can control and monitor home temperatures remotely for energy efficiency.
2. **Smart Light Bulbs:** Bulbs that can be controlled, dimmed, and even change colors using a smartphone app.
3. **Smart Locks:** Electronic locks that can be controlled and monitored remotely, enhancing home security.
4. **Fitness Trackers:** Wearable devices that monitor physical activity, heart rate, and sleep patterns.
5. **Smartwatches:** Watches that can connect to the internet, display notifications, and run various apps.
6. **Smart Refrigerators:** Refrigerators with built-in cameras and sensors to monitor contents and expiration dates.
7. **Smart Cameras:** Security cameras with remote viewing and motion detection capabilities.
8. **Amazon Echo / Google Home:** Voice-activated smart speakers that can perform tasks and answer questions.
9. **Smart Plugs:** Plugs that can turn traditional appliances into smart devices, allowing remote control.
10. **Smart Smoke Detectors:** Smoke detectors that send alerts to your phone in case of emergencies.
11. **Connected Pet Feeders:** Devices that allow you to remotely feed your pets and monitor their activities.
12. **Environmental Sensors:** Sensors that monitor air quality, humidity, and temperature indoors.
13. **Smart Doorbells:** Doorbells with cameras and two-way audio for remote interaction with visitors.
14. **Connected Coffee Makers:** Coffee makers that can be controlled and scheduled remotely.
15. **Smart Water Leak Detectors:** Sensors that send alerts when leaks are detected in your home.
16. **Connected Baby Monitors:** Monitors that provide video and audio feeds of babies to mobile devices.
17. **Smart Garden Sensors:** Sensors that monitor soil moisture and weather conditions for efficient gardening.

18. **Connected Blood Pressure Monitors:** Health devices that track and share blood pressure readings.
19. **Connected Car Diagnostic Tools:** Devices that provide insights into vehicle health and driving behavior.
20. **Smart Home Hubs:** Centralized devices that control various smart devices in a home network.

Printed in the USA
CPSIA information can be obtained
at www.ICGtesting.com
LVHW081313120524
779930LV00007B/1002